Wild HOPE

"A compelling read written with transparency and honesty that highlights dreams fulfilled and challenges faced. This inspirational book addresses the full vocabulary of life—a narrative punctuated with both exclamation marks and question marks. Though Carol carries the pen, it is an account of two people—committed to each other and to God—who prove His faithfulness through both trials and triumph as 'wild hope' blossoms in the soil in which faith is tested. This book blessed us and we are sure it will bless you too."

John and Marilyn Glass. John is general superintendent
of Elim Pentecostal Church (UK) and chairman
of The Evangelical Alliance (UK)

"I desire to live with wild abandon, portraying the same kind of wild hope in Jesus my friend Dr. Carol Alexander has lived out so far spanning four continents. Having grown up a missionary kid, I fully identified with Dr. Alexander as she drew me into each of her experiences from her childhood in South Africa to college in England to ministry with her husband throughout the US, the UK and Australia. But you don't have to be an MK to be inspired to live out a wild hope. Dr. Alexander so skillfully crafts her stories that you are drawn into each experience, nodding your head or tearing up as you identify with heartbreaking pain or soaring heights or seasons of quiet reflection. Most of the life experiences that mold us come from events we never planned—and this honest and powerful account faithfully portrays how God ordains every moment of our lives when we are relentlessly pursuing Him."

Rob Hoskins, president of OneHope, Inc.,
and board chair of **Oral Roberts University**

"*Wild Hope* is contagious! Every chapter makes you wonder what can happen next. There will be tears, and then cheering when *Wild Hope* breaks through. It is applied to life experiences because of faith and trust in God. With still more experiences in Carol's life to come, we look forward to *Wild Hope* Part II."

Sam and Joyce Johnson, executive directors,
Priority One, Minneapolis

"We highly recommend Carol Alexander's book. She beautifully describes the key incidents and stages of her life, allowing the reader to share the warmth and the cold, the sun and the clouds of her experiences. Her compelling narrative challenges her readers to reflect on their own journeys and to focus on that confident 'wild hope' in God who is at work through every season in the life of each Christian believer."

William and Anthea Kay. Dr. William Kay is professor of theology at Glyndwr University, Wales, UK; editor of *Journal of the European Pentecostal Theological Association*; and co-editor of Brill's *Global Pentecostal and Charismatic Studies* series

"Experience is never self-interpreting. Our life stories require regular reflection or they become merely some marks on a calendar of events that detail our lives. The life narrative that Carol provides is uniquely hers, but it is filled with experiences of wonder, amusement, amazement and tragedy which most of us can easily identify with. Her story is personal, but her life has clearly been lived deeply aware of God's guiding trajectory for her entire family. As Carol Alexander tells her personal story, she reflects a life that willingly acknowledges both God's sovereignty and His more than sufficient grace. God's guidance is evident in this family affair that reflects a shared journey of faith following the 'cloud by day and the fire by night.'"

Byron and Lois Klaus. Dr. Byron Klaus is president of the Assemblies of God Theological Seminary

"God always leads us in a right way, not in a comfortable way. Carol Alexander's *Wild Hope* is a memoir of the Lord's right way, even though it meant putting her through experiences that tested her faith and belief sustainability. The milestones of her journey range from personal events through family testings to travels across continents to a variety of ministry callings, ending at North Dakota 'joy.' Each milestone was the Lord's right way, clearly producing His Son's image in her. Her sister's near-death, a son's brush with death as a result of a devastating auto accident, a challenging threat in African missions, challenges in church and school leadership, and the tense moments surrounding a PhD examination. Finally, arrival in Ellendale, North Dakota! Carol teaches us that if we are to glorify God, we must walk like a blind person, trusting the hand and heart of the One who gives us *Wild Hope*. The Reflections are worth the entire book; they encourage *Wild Hope* in the daily walk with Jesus."

Robert and Eileen Cooley. Dr. Robert Cooley is president emeritus, Gordon-Conwell Theological Seminary

Wild HOPE

a memoir

CAROL ANNE ALEXANDER

WESTBOW
PRESS®
A DIVISION OF THOMAS NELSON
& ZONDERVAN

WestBow Press books may be ordered through booksellers or by contacting:

WestBow Press
A Division of Thomas Nelson & Zondervan
1663 Liberty Drive
Bloomington, IN 47403
www.westbowpress.com
1 (866) 928-1240

Because of the dynamic nature of the Internet, any web addresses or links contained in this book may have changed since publication and may no longer be valid. The views expressed in this work are solely those of the author and do not necessarily reflect the views of the publisher, and the publisher hereby disclaims any responsibility for them.

Any people depicted in stock imagery provided by Thinkstock are models, and such images are being used for illustrative purposes only. Certain stock imagery © Thinkstock.

All Scripture quotations are from THE HOLY BIBLE, NEW INTERNATIONAL VERSION®, NIV® Copyright © 1973, 1978, 1984, 2011 by Biblica, Inc.® Used by permission. All rights reserved worldwide.

ISBN: 978-1-4908-9715-8 (sc)
ISBN: 978-1-4908-9716-5 (hc)
ISBN: 978-1-4908-9717-2 (e)

Library of Congress Control Number: 2015911653

Print information available on the last page.

WestBow Press rev. date: 07/24/2015

For Paul,
my fellow sojourner.
I love you with my whole heart—thank you for journeying with me!

And for Mom and Dad.
My gratitude is immeasurable. I love and honor you both!

CONTENTS

FOREWORD BY DJ MCPHAIL

CAROL'S BOOK, *WILD HOPE*, IS a compelling read that I could not put down! She has an incredible way of inviting the reader into her experiences to ignite wonder, hope, and confidence in God's wild plan. I love the way she so poignantly punctuates each chapter with insightful reflections that help you see how your own life is being painted on the canvas of our heavenly Father's providence.

Wild Hope is a journey decorated with colorful and moving images of real-life highs and lows in all their raw invasions, romantic aspirations, and surprising revelations that can so often astound us! Carol's story quickly draws you in to peer through her "window," and while you are engrossed in her compelling journey, you suddenly realize that the reflection on the windowpane has become a mirror, giving you a fresh look at your own dusty memories.

Carol's understanding of God's love and providence has the sun shining through the clouds of even the darkest storms of everyday life. Her authentic and awe-inspiring actual accounts of a life surrendered to the wonder and power of a faithful and yet dangerously unpredictable God inspires *Wild Hope*!

I love what Carol says: "Sometimes there is a depth of beauty beneath that brokenness that is as pure as a crystal stream and runs very deep. Search for it until you find it. Stop to smell the roses and splash in the rain and the mud. Take time to smile at the person in his wheelchair and greet the old, worn face with a lovely soul. Beauty is everywhere if you look for it. God made a stunning world, but the most magnificent of all the things God ever made was you."

I would love every follower of Jesus to pick up on Carol's passion for serving a great big and wholly other God who offers each one of us the adventure of *Wild Hope* in an otherwise bland world often abandoned to fatalism or dead religion.

DJ McPhail, church leader
Liberty Church—Randburg Campus
South Africa

FOREWORD BY KEN WILLIAMSON

IT HAS BEEN MY JOY on so many occasions to sit with Carol Alexander and her husband, Paul, on three of the four continents of the world where they have lived to serve God. In every country they settled in, they were without question in total and joyful obedience to Jesus' call upon their lives. You cannot be in their presence for more than a few minutes and not feel a strong sense of global abandonment to the purposes of God oozing from their lives. It bleeds out of them.

It was the writer Erma Bombeck who said, "When I stand before God at the end of my life, I would hope that I would not have a single bit of talent left, and could say, 'I used everything you gave me.'" This to me sums up Carol's life.

Take a strong sense that Carol knows God is in control of her life, mix it with the learning of the ways of God through the twists and turns of the years, throw in some grit and determination never to quit, add the refusal to be bitter in any circumstance, pour on generosity of heart, inject personal sacrifice for the greater cause, and load on some miraculous provision and the proving of the promises of God, and you will realize that the norm for Carol is an adventure of *wild hope*. Helen Keller said, "Life is either a daring adventure or nothing at all." This is where Carol lives—in a daring, hope-filled adventure.

As you will discover in the pages of this book, although Carol is a highly qualified academic, she, like all of us, is simply a pilgrim, and she has written her story to spur us all on, on the journey of faith and hope we all travel. The writer to Hebrews said, "Let us hold unswervingly to the hope we profess, for he who promised is faithful" (Heb. 10:23).

I commend this book to everyone serious about being a *wild hope* pilgrim.

Ken Williamson, senior pastor
Bethel—London's Riverside Church
London, England

PREFACE

He that lives in hope dances without music.

GEORGE HERBERT

I LIVE ON THE PRAIRIE in the little town of Ellendale, North Dakota. Winter can be brutal, with biting cold winds that hit you with incredible force at fifty mph or more. Nevertheless, whenever I see flocks of snow geese and wild geese heading northward toward the Canadian tundra, I know that spring is on the way, and it fills me with a wild hope for what lies ahead.

Winter for me is the naked season, when the trees shed their leaves and face the elements bare and exposed. As a Christian, that is how I feel in the cold and barren seasons of my life. I never enjoy them, and yet, somehow, it is always in those dismal times of life that I grow and learn the most. I do a lot of shedding; I feel vulnerable, naked and exposed. But I grow! And in the spring I find myself clothed with a new strength and fortitude, and I am equipped to handle the next season that comes my way.

I have come to appreciate the different seasons of life and the uniqueness of each one. When winter passes, the spring has singular beauty that I would never appreciate without having gone through the emptiness of those long, cold months. The stifling heat of summer gives me a longing and appreciation for the cool breezes of the autumn months.

Each season of life has a way of making me appreciate the moment. I sometimes remind myself that the darkest hour is just before the dawn. I would never truly appreciate the splendor of the early morning without having passed through the invasive blackness of the night. As I reflect on my life, I see that some of the darkest nights are the ones that have molded me and made me who I am. And though I did not enjoy the process of going through those experiences, I am a better person because of them.

My life has been full, rich, and diverse. In each moment, and through every season, I have always known that God was there, and even in the most desperate times hope has anchored me.

As I have sat reminiscing for this book, memories shut away for long periods have come creeping back through the crevices of my mind. By no means have I consciously concealed them. They have simply been stored away in the pursuit of living each new day. I am so thankful that cobwebs have not ensnared my memories, and though some of them were dusty and pushed to the far edges of my consciousness, they have thrust their way to the surface and come to the light. Hence this book!

Among some of the happiest memories are also agonizing ones. But even those have been strengthening and enlightening from this perspective in time. As you read about them, I trust your life will be enriched and strengthened.

This book is about how each experience and season has shaped me, making me the person I am today. Truth is wrapped up in various ways. At times it is clothed in some of the most painful and agonizing stories of our lives. But even in the midst of grief, beauty can appear. If you keep your heart open to God through trying times, hope can grow alongside pain and grief, like wild flowers blooming in the desert.

There have been milestones that have shaped me forever, and each one occurred in a specific place that I still recall with crystal clarity. One event, which impacted me forever, was on a beautiful sun-filled day in my childhood home. Another one, which will live with me until the day

I die, happened in a cold, sterile, trauma intensive-care ward. Each of my chapter headings relates a particular place where a watershed event occurred in my life.

Over the years, I have realized how helpful it is for the well-being of my own soul to practice the discipline of contemplation and reflection. Reflection makes us give thoughtful consideration to our past actions so that we can become better human beings. And so, I have a reflective paragraph at the end of each chapter. I hope that you will pause there to allow a time of quiet introspection, considering what God might be saying to you.

I do not live in the past or the future. I live in the present. Living for today makes life exciting. We never know what the day will hold. And life is always interesting when we live with the possibility of a dream being realized.

But life can also throw stuff our way that we never planned for, and it is in those times we become who we are, for good or for bad. Those are moments that can shape us to become people of fortitude.

I do not believe that we are merely victims of our circumstances. We never lose control of situations unless we relinquish that control. It was Viktor Frankl, the German existentialist, who said the last of the human freedoms is man's right to choose his attitude in any and every situation. When life throws things our way that we did not anticipate, we still have the power to make choices, good or bad. We decide. Those moments become turning points that can make us bitter or better. Ultimately, our reaction to those experiences determines our destiny and who we become. We are the guardians of our heart, no one else, so we can never blame others for its condition.

Hope is a choice, which is the golden thread running throughout this book.

Sometimes it is easy to have clarity about how others should lead their lives, but often that certainty is lost on us when it comes to leading and living our own. Hopefully, this book will give some perspective, and as you peer down the corridors of my life, perhaps a light will shine on your own situation, enabling you to respond with hope.

I have not written this book only to tell my story. My desire is that this book will achieve a number of things. I trust it will deal a deathblow to the destructive emotion of fear. Fear is a normal human response to danger and harm, but the problem comes when it consumes us, undermining our faith and robbing us of enjoyment of life. Fear can also be a dream killer. It makes you see why you can't achieve, never allowing you to imagine how you can. We can also have a fear of the unknown and a dread for what might never be. The fear of suffering can be worse than suffering itself. Of all the emotions, fear can be the most destructive and one we need to challenge and confront.

I trust this book will challenge negativity. This is also a harmful emotion that robs us of peace and, like cancer, eats away at our soul, depriving us of joy and freedom. It turns molehills into mountains and stepping-stones into stumbling blocks. Negative thoughts are often irrational, making us susceptible to sin. In that unwholesome frame of negativity, our minds become the Devil's playground. We can spend our days listing our complaints and unraveling a litany of all our problems, or we can develop the habit of cultivating an attitude of gratitude. It is a choice.

I am not using the word *hope* in the way we use it today. Hope often means "wishful thinking." However, I use the word in the biblical sense of Hebrews 11:1, which says, "Now faith is confidence in what we hope for and assurance about what we do not see." In other words, having a certain belief—a confidence. Or as I prefer to say, a *wild hope* in a God who is able to do what we ask Him.

Wherever you are in your journey, my prayer is that you will make space for God in this season of life. If you do this, you will find meaning and joy at each juncture, discovering a God who works in every situation. I do believe that hope is an innate response of the human heart and a defining characteristic of our Christian faith. I pray that this wild hope will seep into your soul and fill you with expectation for your future. The wild geese are on the horizon. Spring is on its way!

Carol Alexander

 *Chapter 1*

Miracle at the Yellow-Brick House

Thou hast created us for Thyself, and our
heart is not quiet until it rests in Thee.

ST. AUGUSTINE

I GREW UP IN A fairly ordinary but extremely colorful family. My paternal grandmother on more than one occasion described in lively tones how our father's family, the Malans, fled the dreadful persecution of Protestants in sixteenth-century France and went to live in Holland, known then as the Dutch Republic. When the Dutch East India Company established the Cape colony in 1652, it offered free citizenship to the many Huguenot families that had escaped to Holland.

My father's ancestors were an intrepid bunch, so they boarded a ship and made the six-month journey across the ocean in the hope of a new and better life at the Cape of Good Hope on Africa's southern tip. The Dutch, the Huguenots, and the German colonists collectively form today's Afrikaner population from whence our family's roots spring.

My grandmother was a stoic lady who had experienced the horror of the British concentration camps during the Anglo-Boer War of 1899 to 1902. She never spoke much about this ordeal other than to mention the cruelty and brutality of the British forces under whose hand she and her own mother suffered profusely. She married my grandfather, who was a successful businessman, but somewhere along the journey of their lives, alcohol became a companion to my grandfather. It held him captive in its cruel grip until their marriage ended in a painful divorce.

My grandmother was a deeply devout woman who had an earnest and sincere faith throughout her lifetime. It was her belief in God that sustained her through the Great Depression and the many other trials she faced as a single parent of four sons and a daughter.

My mother's family had emigrated from the UK, and her father was a quiet but intelligent Welshman who learned to speak Zulu like an African. He met my grandmother, who was significantly younger than he was, extremely beautiful, and a gifted businesswoman. They fell head over heels in love with each other and married shortly after they met. They had two children—a girl and a boy—but unfortunately, Grandpa also became attached to the bottle, and even his deep affection for his stunning bride could not make him give up his addiction.

Grandpa tried on many occasions to quit his habit, but his cravings—followed by bouts of nausea, copious sweating, violent shaking, and anxiety attacks—would send him rushing straight back to the bottle for comfort and relief. Their marriage ended in divorce, but my grandfather lived with an ache in his heart and a love for his bride that never diminished with the passing years. He died loving my grandmother as much as he did on his wedding day.

Although Grandpa married again, it was a platonic relationship that was more a marriage of convenience and companionship than anything else. I didn't understand it when I was a child, but there was sadness in Grandpa's eyes that only went away when he shut them for the final time.

My maternal grandmother died when I was four years old, but her memory is still fresh in my mind. She was a gracious and very distinguished woman who was wholly devoted to her grandchildren. My heart broke when she died, and I still wish she could have shared her life with us.

As destiny would have it my father, a born and bred Afrikaner, fell in love with my mother, whose roots were entrenched in British soil. On a sultry evening at midnight, when the air was thick and stars speckled the blackened sky, my father proposed to my mother outside his house, under a lamppost. There is nothing incredibly romantic about my dad, but I am happy to say that my parents have had a long and happy marriage of sixty-three years at the time of writing this book.

Their alcoholic fathers, and the insecurity and dysfunction that addiction brought to their homes, profoundly affected my parents. There were many occasions when my dad, as a young boy, would take the responsibility of protecting my grandmother and caring for her during some of her vulnerable and trying experiences.

My dad was small, but he was athletic, and he was a champion boxer who became skilled at placing his fist in the appropriate place at the right time. Many of his opponents were rendered powerless after one of his punches. He saved his mother from a devastating blow from an intoxicated relative who was too drunk to know what he was doing.

His sister recalls the occasion when my dad, in a moment of terrifying fury while trying to protect his helpless mother, took this relative by the collar and lifted him in the air, shouting, "If you ever touch my mother again, I will kill you!" No one ever tried to hurt my grandmother again.

I honor my parents for the way they raised us and for how they sought to ensure that we never experienced the instability or insecurity they both lived through.

When I was a young girl, we moved into a lovely three-bedroom, yellow-brick house with a swimming pool to help us cool off on those hot, summer days. Our house stood on an open acre of land, and although it was a simple ranch style, I always thought it smiled in the African sunshine.

I loved my home. Every room was filled with the mischief and laughter of four children, our gregarious Afrikaans dad, and our gentle English mother who lovingly nurtured her family. We always spoke English in our home, despite the fact that my mom and dad were both fluent in Afrikaans.

Life was uncomplicated for a little white South African girl back in the early sixties. I could play safely outside with my friends, mostly unaware of the political tension mounting in those years. Nelson Mandela was a name I sometimes heard adults speak of in hushed tones, and occasionally

I would hear one of them say, "One day this country is going to experience a bloodbath." I had little comprehension of the political structure of our nation and only a vague idea of what apartheid was all about.

My life was fairly sheltered. I went to a suburban school and wore a crisp, clean uniform that our maid washed and ironed daily. Our manservant polished my black lace-up shoes until he could see his reflection in them. Our servants were like extended family, and although they had rooms outside the main house, they were a welcome part of our inner circle.

Our maid, Johanna, kept our house meticulously clean, assuring us that there was no other maid in our neighborhood who could shine wooden floors like she could. She would get down on her knees and rub wax polish on the floors with a cloth, and then she would buff them up with an electric polisher. It was a lengthy process that required patience and endurance.

Joseph ensured that our acre of land was well manicured and watered. When Mom and Dad weren't around, I would send Joseph on trips to the corner store; he was charged with buying me my favorite candy bar. He was always rewarded with one of his choice if he ensured that the secret never got out. To my knowledge, he always kept his side of the bargain.

I never enjoyed Thursdays very much because Johanna had that afternoon off. That meant that we had to help Mom prepare dinner and wash dishes. And in all honesty, dinner was never as good on a Thursday when Johanna wasn't around to help.

Unfortunately, Johanna spent many of her Thursday afternoons intoxicated as she gulped down copious amounts of home-brewed millet beer. This meant that Fridays were choice days to keep out of Johanna's path, because she had a huge headache and a dark mood to match it. However, once her hangover passed, she was amiable and kind and in every way one of the extended members of our household.

I was wrapped up in my safe, secluded world and lived in a bubble, oblivious to the fact that black people had been taken out of urban areas and forced into homelands and townships. It was under the Group Areas Act that urban and rural areas were divided into zones in which only one racial group could live; all other people had to be displaced. The cold, bare facts are that black people had to move under threat or by force.

I was unaware that they were deprived of citizenship and that the government segregated education, medical services, and public services. To every extent and purpose, blacks were considered inferior human beings.

It would be wonderful to say that this unconscionable injustice troubled me and stirred me to advocacy on behalf of the oppressed. But that would be crediting my naïve, young self with a nonexistent piety. I remained blissfully ignorant of their plight and simply reveled in the advantages afforded a little white girl.

Today, I feel ashamed of those unjust laws that robbed people of their rights, dignity, and freedom. Noted theologian Dietrich Bonheoffer's words echo in my mind, reminding me, "We are not to simply bandage the wounds of victims beneath the wheels of injustice, we are to drive a spoke into the wheel itself." I look back now aware of the sheer lunacy of apartheid and the incredible price that has been paid for that policy, but back then I was just an ordinary South African girl growing up oblivious to what was taking place around her. The fact never entered my head that small shantytowns with inadequate housing, no electricity, and insufficient water were just across the way from the beautiful jacaranda trees that lined our pristine, paved walkways and manicured lawns.

My parents regularly attended the Methodist church in Bedfordview; it was only a ten-minute drive from our home. They took us to church most Sundays, and although I found the preaching boring, it was an occasion for my imagination to run wild and explore different parts of the world. This was one time when I knew that I would be uninterrupted as my mind roamed and rummaged in faraway places.

As the preacher rambled on in his monotone voice, my mind explored the Dickensian cobbled pathways of London, the neon-lit streets of New York City, and the narrow rainy roads and boulevards of Paris and beyond.

I had always been fascinated with different places and cultures, and this innate desire for exploring the world was growing inside of me. Little did I realize that even then God was nudging me towards my destiny.

Church was a satisfying hour for me as my mind explored different parts of the world, and even though the preacher and his sermons were unpalatable and offensive to my young ears, I was decidedly interested in God. I said my prayers daily and had a deep sense that God was infinitely bigger and more powerful than anyone or anything.

My first clear memory of an encounter with God was when I was thirteen years old. Our maid, Johanna, and our manservant, Joseph, had gone on vacation for a month, so my older sister, Gaille, and I were helping Mom do the washing and cleaning, and my younger brother, Geoff, was working in the yard. Gaille was polishing the dining room furniture while I helped Mom hang washing on the line.

It was a beautiful southern-hemisphere December morning; the sky was ink blue and the earth smelled deliciously fresh from an early morning rain shower. The gentle breeze and warm summer sun would often dry the laundry in under an hour, leaving it crisp and smelling fresh.

As the gentle rays of the morning sun streamed down on us, I heard a clear, penetrating voice in my head, which I knew instinctively was God speaking to me.

"Tracy is drowning in the pool."

Each word had a staccato-like precision that hammered into my head with unrelenting force.

My little sister, Tracy, was twenty-two months old at that time and the baby of the family. Not for a moment did I doubt that God had interrupted my thoughts to get my attention, and although I had no personal relationship with Him, I knew even at that young age that it was His voice I heard.

I had a little conversation with Him then and there. It wasn't lengthy, probably only a second or two. I said naively, "If I tell Mom that You told me Tracy is drowning, she will think I am crazy." So I simply asked, "Mom, where is Tracy?" I hoped this would rouse her curiosity enough to do something about the imminent tragedy occurring as my little sister was slowly deprived of oxygen in the pool at the end of our yard.

Mom casually replied that Tracy was with Gaille in the dining room.

I wanted to scream, "No! She is drowning. God told me!" Instead, I went to confirm her words, rushing to the dining room to see if I could find Tracy. Of course, I knew she wouldn't be there. And all this time the seconds were ticking away as my baby sister drowned in our swimming pool, life slowly seeping from every cell in her tiny frame as she was robbed of air.

I ran back out as quickly as my legs could carry me, shouting with sheer desperation, "Mom, she's nowhere in the house." The urgency in my voice caught her attention, and as her own intuition kicked in, I saw her running towards the pool with the terminal velocity of an Olympic runner. She dove in and came out of the pool dripping wet, utterly distraught, sobbing as she carried a lifeless two-year-old in her arms.

I had always had a marvelous pair of lungs, and today I needed them. My older sister was smaller than me, but she was much stronger, and she often used her strength to keep me exactly where she needed and wanted me to be. My only defense against her unassailable power was to scream at the top of my lungs. I had a fair bit of practice under my belt, so much so that at thirteen I had an awfully good pair of lungs. On this particular day they came to good use.

When I saw Mom with the lifeless form of my baby sister, I screamed frantically, "God, help us," over and over again as I ran around and around the yard in a total frenzy. The neighbor next door heard my screams and thought for a moment that we kids were having a brawl.

I am not sure how many octaves my voice climbed, but as she listened to the terror rising in my voice, she realized it was something more and came quickly to see what was happening.

There was utter desperation in my mother's eyes; agony was etched on her face as she ran up the driveway with my sister's limp body. When she reached our neighbor, she threw the lifeless form into her arms and rushed off to call for help.

Her hands trembled with a violence that frightened me and tears rolled down her face as she stumbled to the phone in our hallway to call the ambulance.

My older sister, Gaille, rushed off at lightning speed to see if the nurse that lived up the street was at home. (Alas, she was not.)

Our neighbor carefully placed Tracy's limp body on the grass and laid her on her back. There was a bluish tinge around her lips, and although it looked as if she was sleeping, it was clear that her chest was not moving up and down as it should have been if she was breathing.

She lay on the carpet of green, her tiny frame motionless.

I felt a numbness creep over my body as I looked at my little sister's lifeless form. There was a burning sensation at the back of my throat, and although I tried my utmost to swallow my tears, I could not. They prickled in the corner of my eyes, stinging them, until suddenly, without warning, they began to flow down my cheeks.

Our neighbor, Mrs. Beneke, wasted no time as she tilted Tracy's head back and raised her chin. She pressed her mouth over Tracy's lips and forced one breath after another into her tiny lungs. I stood there as hot tears streamed down my face and wet the collar of my pretty floral blouse. I was vaguely aware of the silhouette of my young brother, Geoff, but my focus was on the neighbor and my little sister, who was at her mercy.

I watched closely as Mrs. Beneke pressed her two fingers on Tracy's tiny breastbone and pushed down in quick succession. She was giving my sister CPR, striving desperately to save her life. She would place her ear against Tracy's mouth to listen for her breath—feeling for the flutter of life on her cheek. Nothing! Then she'd checked for her pulse. Nothing! Back to CPR and then pressing her mouth against Tracy's lips, forcing air from her own lungs back into Tracy's. It seemed like an eternity as I watched helplessly while our neighbor worked frantically to save my sister's life.

She lay there frighteningly still. Her body was limp and lifeless. I stood there, aware that my little sister lay in the throes of death and I was helpless to do anything.

Our neighbor kept on going, forcing air and checking for a pulse. She was relentless in her pursuit. She would breathe, check for my sister's breath, look for a pulse, and breathe into her little lungs again.

The air around me hung thick and heavy, with a stillness that was electric. I could feel our neighbor's anxiety and I could hear the thud of my own heart. I felt as if the angel of death was standing right there, waiting in readiness to clutch another victim.

Eventually, after what felt like forever, but could only have been minutes, Mrs. Beneke found a pulse. Suddenly a muffled cry broke through the piercing silence, and my little sister began to spew up water and cough. She was breathing. She was alive.

Mom hurried outside to the muffled sound of Tracy's cries. Her voice cracked as she cried out, "Thank you, thank you!" The relief that spread across her face was such a contrast to the sheer agony of a few minutes earlier that I wanted to laugh and cry all at once. I know now that when Death comes to the doorstep of a loved one, its sinister breath curling at his or her neck, and then is vanquished, you are infused with a gratitude so immense that your dear one has escaped its cold clutches that nothing can ever be quite the same again.

Mom and Mrs. Beneke both rushed to the car to get Tracy to the doctor as quickly as they could. Fortunately, a well-qualified medical practitioner, Dr. Barnard (cousin to the late Dr. Chris Barnard, the famous surgeon who performed the first heart transplant in the world), lived down the street from us.

Mom headed straight to his house, giving no thought to the possibility of interrupting him on his morning off. Tracy was wrapped in a yellow cotton blanket and all I could see were her little bare feet and ten pink toes hanging limply out from underneath. Somewhere between the house and pool her black patent-leather shoes had fallen off and her woolen socks edged with fine white lace had gone astray.

Her eyes fluttered open as they got her into the car, and I heard her whimpering softly. "Can I go with you, Mom?" I appealed as they jumped into the car. Mom shook her head and assured me she would be home as soon as possible.

Gaille, Geoff, and I sat quietly on the outside step of the kitchen door looking at the patch of grass where our little sister had lain just minutes earlier. We never said a word. The three of us were all too stunned at the morning's sudden and dismal turn of events. We were physically exhausted from running in different directions looking for help.

But the emotional trauma was what had taken the greatest toll.

Our happy home had been seriously threatened by a near tragedy that we could never have anticipated. As we sat on the cold concrete step, there was only stillness. I could hear my siblings breathing and it was comforting. I listened closely for more sounds as my ears began to tune once more into the world around me. Suddenly, I heard the birds singing, and somehow I knew everything would be all right.

My mom later told us what transpired at Dr. Barnard's home. Mrs. Beneke banged loudly on the doctor's front door. The thunderous rapping must have dismayed him; he came swiftly to the door and opened it with alarm. When he saw my poor, bedraggled mother with a helpless disheveled toddler in her arms, he quickly ushered them into his living room, where he laid Tracy down on his soft and luxurious couch and started to unbutton her drenched dress. In a professional, but concerned, voice he asked Mom, "How long was she in the pool?"

Mom could only fathom a guess that she had been under the water for up to five minutes. That caused him a fair amount of anxiety and he ran for his stethoscope to listen to her heart and lungs. But after a thorough checkup he declared her to be well enough to be taken home.

I remember Mom returning with Tracy. Her auburn hair was still damp, but her green eyes shone out from under the blanket and seemed to say "I'm back! Everything will be all right." Her little cheeks had some color in them, and she gave us all a sweet smile, assuring us that the rooms in our yellow-brick house would once more be filled with laughter.

We had not fully comprehended at that point the extent of the miracle that occurred. Now, as I reflect on things, I realize how God was so evidently present through that frightening event. You can only imagine how amazed we were when we later learned that the day before Tracy's near drowning, Mrs. Beneke had come home from church and, after their traditional Sunday roast dinner, sat down to read the *Sunday Times* as she did week by week. She had come across a cartoon strip in the newspaper that described step by step how to do CPR. As she was turning the page, she felt a strong impression: *"Read this caption, you will need it one day."* She went back to the cartoon and slowly and carefully read how to resuscitate someone. Little did she realize that early on Monday morning a desperate situation would require the use of those skills.

At the dinner table that night, we bowed our heads and said grace. In simple childlikeness I thanked God for giving Tracy back to us. There was a resounding "Amen!" from every member of our family. Once again, joy and laughter filled the rooms of our home.

That night, as stars in the Milky Way shimmered in the heavens, we went peacefully to bed. Our hearts were glad as we anticipated waking to another glorious sunrise with its peachy-mauve hues filtering through the windows of our yellow-brick house and filling us with wild hope for the morrow.

Reflection

As is evident from my reminiscence, there were a number of circumstances that coincided to save my sister's life. God had organized events to culminate in this amazing miracle. His voice in my head, the cartoon strip in the newspaper, the neighbor responding to my cry for help—every situation had His fingerprints all over it.

There can be numerous complications from a near drowning. A lack of oxygen can cause brain damage even if breathing is restored. Water seeping into the lungs can produce inflammation of the lining, which leads to acute respiratory problems. Tracy was monitored for forty-eight hours with no complications or negative side effects from the near tragedy.

I had no personal knowledge of God at that time, but I knew beyond a shadow of a doubt that God intervened and our family witnessed a miracle. He had revealed to me that He was right there with our family when we needed Him. And now my heart was restless for Him; I had an insatiable hunger, a yearning and emptiness that I longed for Him to fill. God's fingerprints on that December day left an indelible mark in my soul, and my heart overflowed with a deep longing and an inexplicable hope that He would make Himself known to me.

When I look back over my life, I am amazed to see how God pursued me. As Francis Thompson wrote in his famous poem "Hound of Heaven," God never ceases to chase after our souls. In His unhurried pace He pursued me with relentless grace and my heart was tender and ready to respond. The God of heaven was going after me, hounding me, and my heart could no longer resist. I was ready for the adventure!

Perhaps you have been aware of God's involvement in your life, but have never taken the opportunity to acknowledge it. Why not take a moment now to pause and reflect on those times. If you have not yet discovered His purpose, take time to acknowledge His hand in your life and give Him your future.

Maybe you are reading this book because God is trying to get your attention, pursuing you with relentless grace. If your soul is feeling that gentle pressure, urging you to turn to Him, I encourage you: do not resist Him.

Open your heart and allow it to be filled with wild hope.

 *Chapter 2*

A Heart Made Whole
Inside a Canvas Tent

There is a God shaped vacuum in the heart of every
man which cannot be filled by any created thing, but
only by God, the Creator, made known through Jesus.

BLAISE PASCAL

MY POOR MOM—I AM NOT sure how she coped with the sprightly, inquiring child I was. So many questions swam around my brain, and the muddled beliefs floating in my head were beginning to demand answers. I had three other siblings—an older sister, a younger brother, and our little miracle sister, Tracy. However, I was the one always probing Mom with philosophical questions about God and life.

I remember asking her one day, "Mom, what happens when we die?" She stopped what she was doing and looked at me with a slightly bewildered expression, then sighed abruptly. At this phase in her life she had no personal faith. She always tried to answer my questions as best as she possibly could, but I sensed she was struggling with this one.

Meeting my gaze, she responded, "Well, if we have the right religion we go to heaven, and if we have the wrong one we go to hell."

I was not anticipating that response. And though I realized from

Mom's body language that she was done with my inquest, she had just evoked another question.

I could sense her discomfort level rising and saw the vaguely annoyed expression on her face as I asked, "Mom, do we have the right religion?" Her reply troubled me even more.

"I don't know, darling. We will have to wait until we die to find out."

I felt as if an icy wind slapped my face.

I was disturbed. This was a problem for a ten-year-old! Risky business, waiting until I died to find out if I would be permitted entrance to the pearly gates, with angels singing and welcoming me into God's presence, or the fiery furnace below, with demons spitting out sulfur and venom while announcing my eternal damnation. (Sadly, this was my perspective of eternity.)

I left my mom convinced there was something profoundly wrong with her answer. It left my heart and mind troubled. Young as I was, I could not accept what she had told me, and so I continued to pray to a God I did not comprehend, longing for Him to reveal Himself to me.

It is amazing that I had gone to church and Sunday school almost all of my life (albeit a decidedly short one at that stage) yet had no concept of what the Bible said about life or death.

But of course a gracious, loving God sees the hearts of those who are searching for Him, and He will always respond. In the meantime I blithely continued my young life in South Africa.

Johannesburg was the city where I was born and spent my early life. Even though it is only one hundred miles south of the Tropic of Capricorn, do not mistakenly think that it is bathed in tropical sunlight all the year through. The city lies about six thousand feet above sea level and can get bitterly cold in winter. The days are warm with indigo blue skies, but at night the temperatures drop below freezing. No homes have central heating, so everyone complains bitterly during the three months of winter. Nor are South African homes well insulated; the cold air from outside makes its unwelcome entrance through the sheet-thin, single-pane windows. Beautiful, big verandahs are a feature of many South African homes, providing the necessary shade and respite from the sun during those hot summer months, but they are also barriers preventing the sun's rays from penetrating the homes during the cold months.

At night, my siblings and I would sit in our warm flannel pajamas, wrapped in wooly blankets, all huddled around a small electric heater.

Likewise, schools were never heated, which made winters quite miserable leaving everyone pining for summer.

Still, I loved my city; it had a rich and exciting history that seemed to permeate the atmosphere with hope. It wasn't as beautiful as Cape Town with its magnificent Table Mountain, but it was booming economically and in the late 1960s it boasted the Hillbrow Tower, one of the tallest in Africa.

But it was the people who made the city what it was. There was a vibrancy in the air, the entrepreneurial, pioneering spirit of men and women, and a sense that nothing was impossible. No dream could be thwarted, no idea could be stifled, and no hand could be stopped. Anything and everything was possible. Perhaps it was this visionary atmosphere that filled my heart from an early age and gave me a desire to make a difference in my world.

The city of Johannesburg was established as a result of the discovery of gold, and it quickly became one of the richest goldfields in the world. Back in the late 1800s, as men dug for the shiny nuggets, earth was excavated from underground, processed, and the gold removed. The remainder of earth was then piled on top of the land. These goldmine dumps were a unique feature of Johannesburg when I was growing up.

I remember during the winter months, the wind would blow the fine, powdery dust from those golden mounds into our homes. Our maid grumbled continuously at the amount of work this cream-colored sand produced, and it seemed that a duster was never far from her hand. Today turf and shrub cover these buttery mounds, disguising the ugliness of man's creation and preventing pollution of the cities surrounding them.

On one particular winter morning, as the sun shyly attempted to push through the clouds, I sat at my little wooden desk in school pondering a young people's church camp that I had been invited to attend. Our Methodist community was planning a trip to Scottburgh, a little coastal town situated on the mouth of the Mpambanyi River, just thirty-six miles south of Durban. The camp was organized for two weeks in the hot, summer month of December. I desperately wanted to go, but only if my best friend, Janet, went.

Thankfully, after one of our Sunday morning church services, Janet's mom and mine decided it would be a great idea to send us both to camp. We were at the start of those challenging teenage years, and they felt that some time away from family would be good for the two of us. And what better place for two impressionable young girls to be nurtured and helped than a church camp? Our two moms had great expectations for their young daughters, but I don't think they were anticipating the outcome of that church camp.

The winter months seemed to drag on endlessly. But as the bare trees gradually clothed themselves in the soft, pastel shades of spring, our excitement about the church camp could not be contained anymore than the buds forcing their way through the barren branches.

Eventually, spring gave way to summer, scenting the air with the delicious fragrances of jasmine and honeysuckle, leaving Janet and me filled with anticipation for the adventure ahead. The thought of leaving the dust of Johannesburg for the Indian Ocean with its cool, clean sea breezes was tantalizing indeed. I had a deep innate sense that something special was awaiting me.

In late December, our two families drove to Johannesburg Central Station. It was the first time I had been apart from my family, which made me feel very grown-up. We said our good-byes and boarded the overnight train that would take us through Durban and onto Scottburgh.

I still remember the beautiful, warm glow of the amber wood that framed the windows and doors of the train, the faded brown-leather seats with the honey, leathery smell that delighted your nostrils as you entered your compartment. There was something wonderful and charming about those old trains; they had a character and an ambience that invited you into their apricot glow and cozy atmosphere.

The train trundled along the tracks, and although the trip took endless hours, you felt hugged and secure in the warm atmosphere, which made you almost dread the journey coming to an end.

Modern trains seem dull and sterile in comparison. With all the marvelous advances of our century, I think we have lost the ability to take time, savor the moment, and relish the experience. Those old train trips forced you to stop, breathe, and enjoy.

We got onto the train with our suitcases and brown paper bags bulging with sandwiches, boiled eggs, sausages, and candy. We ate with relish and excitement as we gradually moved out of Johannesburg, through Germiston, and onto Durban.

The ticket master called to check our tickets, followed by the bedding steward, who came to our compartment to make up our beds with crisp, white linen sheets and grey woolen blankets. As he made our beds, he chattered to us about our adventure ahead and assured us that a good night of rest would prepare us for it.

Despite the encouraging words, Janet and I slept remarkably little through the night as the train rolled along, but eventually the noise and swaying motion lulled us into a short but luscious sleep.

The next morning, as the sun broke through the African sky, tinting it with amber hues, we could see we were meandering down emerald hills towards Durban. South Africa is a land of magnificent beauty. It groans and travails under the burdens of past guilt, but at the same time it oozes with optimism and wild hope for the future. It is a land of extremes and contrasts, but despite all of its incongruences it is a land I love dearly.

We stopped at all the little stations to let off passengers along the way until we arrived at our destination in Scottburgh. And then followed two weeks of delightful diversions.

We ate good food, drank too much Coca-Cola, and consumed copious amounts of my favorite lime ice cream. We swam in the warm Indian Ocean and tried desperately to avoid flirtatious boys—who, having left their inhibitions at home, were far too assertive in the sunshine and carefree summer holiday season. Every boy's quest that season seemed to be capturing a pretty girl, and some girls were silly enough to succumb to their wily ways.

We had fun! And finally, as camp came to an end, we were all called to a meeting in the army-green canvas tent that stood prominently in the center of the grounds.

On that warm, sultry Friday evening, just before our departure the next day, we sang some of the familiar camp songs that I loved singing despite the fact that many of the words had little meaning or spiritual significance.

When we finished, Archie, our camp director, told us that some of the young people on camp wanted to tell us their stories of how Jesus had changed their lives. I didn't know that Jesus got involved in our lives, and I certainly did not understand how He could *change* a life. What did that mean? God was great, but He was far away, too transcendent to be involved with mere mortals.

I understood the concept of "Creator of the universe," but I thought He was uninvolved with His creation, leaving us to fend for ourselves and to get on with writing our own story.

Could the God of creation really be involved in all the intricate details of my insignificant story?

The idea that the Creator of the universe was holding the world together and sustaining it and His creation was mind boggling. The concept of an infinite God fit my framework, but that He could be involved in a personal relationship with me was radical indeed. To be honest, I had never heard this kind of language before, and it enthralled me. I sat captivated for the next hour as I listened to these kids express in faltering, nervous, yet passionate tones how they had become Christ followers. The air was charged and the silence intensified as we listened to their stories.

What I heard about Jesus that day did not fit my mental framework, but it rang true with my heart. I had watched some of these young people over the past couple of weeks, noting how different their lives were from my own. I knew then that it was Jesus in their lives and their stories that made the difference, and I found Him beautiful and irresistible.

This is it; this is exactly what I have been looking for, I thought to myself. I knew with every fiber of my being that I wanted Jesus to be part of my life. I wanted the peace that He promised in the Bible as well as the hope He offered to live each day.

What captured my imagination was that Jesus did not only offer hope for life after I died, He offered hope for life before I died. The assurance that when I died I would go to heaven was simply another bonus of this new life.

Though they stumbled over their words, somehow those young people managed to articulate what the gospel was all about: Jesus loved me so much that He had given His life for me on a cross. He wanted a personal relationship with me, and He wanted to be a part of my life.

This beautiful story was not some imaginary fairy tale or delightful fancy; it was as real as the people sharing their stories with us that day. It gripped my heart and my imagination and stopped me in my tracks, sending me in a whole new direction.

On that hot January day in 1969, I knew that Jesus was the answer. He was the One to fill the vacuum in my life. My heart had been restless, questioning, troubled; I wanted Him to fill and quiet it.

Archie asked if anyone wanted to invite Jesus into his or her life that day. Without a moment of hesitation I responded, as did Janet. Archie took us aside to a quiet spot. As we prayed, I opened my heart to Jesus, asking Him to live inside of me, to take my hand and journey with me through life. From that moment on, I knew I never wanted to live one more day of my life without His hand in mine.

And that was the day my new life began! From that day to this I have never stopped imagining how this incredible gospel story can transform human lives. It is this imagination that propels me to do what I do—to sacrifice houses, land, and security so that this amazing story can bring healing to the hurting, hope to the hopeless, and restoration to the broken.

Archie told me later that all the camp leaders had prayed constantly throughout those few weeks for me. For some reason, they had felt that God had a purpose for my life. They had been burdened to pray specifically that I would become a Christ follower.

That day Jesus filled the God-shaped vacuum inside me. I felt God's peace wrap around me like a warm blanket emitting His warmth and love. Of all the decisions I have made in my life, that is the one I have never regretted. On that day, a new, wild hope filled my heart.

Reflection

I lost touch with Janet as we went our separate ways. I know she professed to wanting Jesus, but I have often wondered where her spiritual journey took her. I marvel at the way God orchestrates events in our lives to achieve His purpose. I see my life as a tapestry that the Master Weaver is perpetually working on. As He joins the dots to weave the threads of my life together, He smiles at the plan He has in mind.

I feel secure in His handiwork, knowing that He will never make a mistake as He completes the work He started. It gives me hope to know that God is intimately involved in every detail of my life—so much so that the Bible says He knows how many hairs I have on my head.

As the years have passed, I find myself clinging ever tighter to Him, longing ever more to feel His arms enfolding me. It is a comforting place to be and one that fills me with joy.

If your life is empty, I suggest that you say a simple prayer to Jesus. Prayer is simply talking to God as you would a friend. You can bare your heart to Him. One thing I am certain of: if you do open your heart to Jesus, He will not disappoint you. He hears the faintest cry and can fill the emptiest heart with wild hope!

Chapter 3

God's Voice in a Little Lilac Bedroom

What God says is best, is best, though all the men in the world are against it.

JOHN BUNYAN

I WAS EXCITED TO GET home from camp and share my newfound faith with my family. This new hope of salvation, resurrection, and eternal life that I had embraced were bubbling inside of me. I was eager to tell my family how a commitment to Jesus was not simply a ticket to heaven but a hope for today as well as for our present world. This hope could come alive in our community and in our ailing nation. I was bursting to tell them that Jesus was the answer to every problem!

My mind still holds the image of the old Johannesburg train station. The huge, black, round station clock suspended in midair and the rhythmic ticking reminding us that time waits for no one. Parents and children waiting on the platform as the train slowly shuffles in filled with passengers eager to be reunited with their families. My family was there among the many, with broad smiles and warm hugs to welcome me back home. It was a joyous moment.

On the drive home from the train station, I poured out my heart about my wonderful, discovery of hope in Jesus. I couldn't contain my joy. I felt infused with a new and vibrant energy.

Silence and blank stares were all I got. Still in his seat, with his hands on the steering wheel, Dad sat rigid as an iron pole, only his eyes moved as he drove. As I watched him, I could see his shoulders twitching.

No one said a word. It looked as if my mom and siblings were frozen in the moment, sitting stiffly like toy soldiers. But I jabbered on, filling the silence with my enthusiasm and jubilance. Nothing could stifle my joy, even though the silence stretched on until we arrived home.

And so the days followed. My family appeared nonchalant about my commitment to Jesus. Truth be told, we never know how God is working in the life of another. Clearly, I did not realize God was disturbing the chemistry of my mom's soul and changing her heart. What appeared as a cool and disinterested take on my conversion was actually nothing of the sort.

God was tinkering in Mom's heart and her hunger for an authentic relationship with Jesus was intensifying. It was not long before Mom became a Christ follower, and my sister Gaille followed shortly after.

My dad was a keen golfer, which being interpreted meant that he was on the golf course every weekend. He had a good golfing buddy by the name of Mickey, and they both enjoyed their Sunday game. Mickey's wife, Shirley, was a Christ follower—a fact of which my dad was totally unaware.

One day Mickey invited Dad to bring all of us to a picnic so our families could meet each other. My dad has always been an energetic, fun-loving man, and so he readily accepted the invite. Oh, how I marvel at the way God works. He is so clever!

The day of the picnic arrived and thankfully the rain held off. Our house was a flurry of happy activity as we scurried to pack our chicken-salad sandwiches, bags of potato chips, and Mom's delicious lemon-meringue tart, as well as copious amounts of Coca-Cola to quench our thirst. Our spirits were elevated by the beautiful weather, the anticipation of good food, and a day of relaxation.

Instantly we connected with Mickey's wife, Shirley, finding her fervor for Jesus infectious. We were aware that Mickey and Dad were eavesdropping on our conversation as we spoke about Jesus, and it appeared to leave both of them feeling slightly uncomfortable, wondering if bringing their families together had been such a good idea after all. The picnic had certainly not taken the route they anticipated.

Soon after that, Shirley invited us to attend a meeting at Fairview Assembly of God in Johannesburg. The church at Fairview had a rich history. A young, intrepid Irishman, Fred Mullin pioneered it in the late 1930s. He had an evangelistic and healing gift, and Fairview grew rapidly under his leadership.

I remember walking into the church for the very first time. Beautiful, royal-blue velvet drapes lined the back wall of the church. A plain, carved wooden podium stood prominently in the middle of the platform, while Pastor Louis Potgieter—rocking back and forth behind the podium with his beaming smile and large, rotund frame—energetically waved his arms as he led the congregation in song. The people sang with gusto. I was captivated! I had never heard singing like this in a church. People really meant what they sang.

Fairview was by no means the perfect church, but it became my church, and I loved it.

I have always marveled at how churches, including Fairview, seem to have a way of attracting dysfunctional people. But then, isn't that what Jesus did? He attracted the marginalized, oppressed, sick, and lonely. Fairview was no different. Honestly, I encountered situations at this church that I never anticipated.

I was naïve, thinking that all Christ followers would live their lives in obedience to the Bible, loving each other and living together in perfect harmony. How wrong I was. I saw flawed leadership and encountered Christians who were less than kind and sometimes intentionally hurtful. But warts and all, it was where I belonged, and I needed my community to grow into the person God had destined for me to be.

To use a metaphor, some churches are nurseries. A cacophony fills the air with the sounds of crying and laughter. Dirty diapers, bad odors, mess, and chaos are the order of the day. But there is life—unlike a cemetery, where there is order, silence, and serenity, but the atmosphere is filled with death. I know where I would rather be. The nursery may be chaotic, filled with squabbles and tears, but it is a vibrant place of growth and life.

How like the church. No, I should say that is how churches should be. Of all the characteristics a church should replicate, growth and life should be the two most identifiable features. Unfortunately, this is not always the case, and many Western churches are places where steady decline and imminent death are at hand.

Many people become disgruntled with the church, and unfortunately, some become bitter wearing the emblem of cynicism. Too often I have heard this common refrain from resentful people: "I will never darken the doors of a church again because it is full of hypocrites."

That may be true, but we must look at the bigger picture.

The church is a gathering place for people. Many of them, sadly, are hurting—some of them dysfunctional and in a lifelong process of becoming whole. In this community, we rub shoulders with other folks who have flaws just like us, and in so doing we learn from each other; we heal from our hurts, grow in our faith, and hopefully become better, stronger Christians.

It is in this organic, noisy, messy, chaotic community that we laugh and rejoice when things go well. But it is also the place where we hold each other tight and weep together in our desperate moments. Yes, at times, we fail one another dismally, but we are the church, which is why we stick together through the disorder and confusion of life.

I have always believed in the importance of belonging to a church family. God designed for us to be in community and it troubles me that some Christians choose not to belong anywhere. There is no perfect church in the world, but it is God's family, and I believe it is where our faith can grow as we worship and mingle with bruised, hurting, and imperfect people like us.

Despite hearing some boring sermons and singing some silly songs, I loved my church family. I remember our worship leader leading his favorite chorus. It went something along the lines of Christians being as happy as birds upon a tree. When it got to the refrain, he would put his hand behind his ear and tilt his head toward the congregation for a response—to which everyone happily chirped back, "Tweet, tweet." We would then go full steam singing the next stanza about being contented and happy.

I get embarrassed just thinking about that song and the silly refrain "Tweet, tweet." But we sang it with enthusiasm and gusto as we worshipped Jesus with all our hearts.

My dad didn't know what lay ahead of him the day he said yes to a picnic. I can just see God sitting in heaven, smiling as He wove His plan together. He is masterful! It wasn't long before Dad, Geoff, and my sister Tracy became Christ followers as well.

My sister Gaille and I attended youth meetings with Shirley's two daughters. I remember the first one we went to. We walked in from the side street and entered through the black, wrought-iron gate, down a short concrete path, and into the minor hall where the meeting was held. I saw a blond-haired, blue-eyed, charismatic young man leading the meeting. Instantly he caught my attention. There was something about him that appealed to me—his youthful confidence, his infectious smile, and his delightful effervescence. I think I loved him from that moment. His name was Paul.

I was a shy sixteen-year-old with a pale-olive complexion that highlighted my long blonde hair and framed my green eyes.

Those were the days when boys pursued girls and made all the advances. It was considered somewhat common for a girl to be in any way suggestive or flirtatious. The general practice was that no girl should ever chase after a boy. And that was certainly one social norm I was intent on keeping.

There were no cell phones, no texting or social media, to assist boys in their pursuit of a particular girl. Those were the days when they had to be bold and go up to a girl and have a conversation with her to get her attention. These societal rules and norms were adhered to by most.

Young people today may think this approach to dating is archaic and ridiculous, but there was an innocence about those times. And those were the days courting couples sat and spoke to each other in cafés, drinking milk shakes and eating hamburgers. With no phones to hide behind, they had to look into each other's eyes and converse to find out things about the other person. They did not discover facts about them on Facebook or via any other form of social media. Novel indeed!

Paul assures me that he tried desperately to get my attention. Perhaps I was naïve or simply misread the signals, but I didn't think he was interested in me. I was shy, unsure of myself, and afraid because this boy was invading my thoughts more than I wanted him to.

One night after the church service, he struck up a conversation with a far too pretty girl. It was her first visit to our church, and somehow she caught his attention. He spent what seemed to me an eternity chatting with her. I was devastated.

"Well, that's it," I thought, "So, he doesn't like me!" I left the church that night a picture of despair, my chin on the ground and my heart in my shoes.

When I reached home, I retreated to the quiet space of my lilac bedroom. After what seemed like hours of lying in my bed feeling sorry for myself, I drifted off to sleep. I know I was sleeping, but it was light, the early phases before that deep and luxurious stage.

I don't think it had been very long before I heard a voice penetrating my mind. My name was called twice.

"Carol . . . Carol . . ."

I responded. "Yes, Lord." I knew this was God's voice because it was unlike any human voice.

I then heard ten simple, life-altering words: *"Soon, very soon, Paul will be yours and all yours."*

And then I fell into that deep and wonderfully delectable stage of sleep. I knew innately that this experience was a turning point in my life.

The next morning the sun streamed in through my windows. Doves were cooing outside, and as I lay in bed watching the wind blow through the leaves of the old willow tree at the end of the yard, a wild hope filled my heart for what God had in store for me. I knew from that day that I would marry Paul.

I only wished God would tell him and everyone else—that would have been very helpful to me!

But I had to leave it to the Lord to convince Paul of His plan. I hoped God understood that I would not be helping Him to achieve His purpose because I was a shy and timid little South African girl who had every intention of keeping her good reputation intact. There was no way I would chase a boy and be called a flirt. If God could speak to my heart, He would have to convince Paul. I was ready for what God had in store. However, there was no way in which I was assisting Him in accomplishing His plan.

Reflection

I have always been thankful that our Christian faith is different than other religions. We have a God who speaks to us and longs to have a relationship with us His children. He is not a distant and uninvolved God.

I have only heard God's audible voice a few times in my life. Perhaps God needed to get my attention because my faith was new and I was still immature and unsure.

As I have grown in my faith, though, I have learned to recognize God's voice in different ways. He still speaks to me, but often I hear His voice in whispers, or He nudges me in a particular direction or simply prompts me to action. I have also heard God's voice direct me in a specific way or encourage me through reading His Word.

God wants a relationship with all of His children; we simply need to open our hearts to Him and listen for that voice that can be an audible, still, small whisper or a nudge or a prompt.

I encourage you to open your heart and your ears to listen to God speak. Saint Benedict said to listen with the ear of your heart. As you do this, you will experience God in a richer way as He prompts you through His Word or nudges you with encouragement from others or whispers to you in that still voice that Elijah spoke about.

I was willing and ready to hear God's voice for the next phase of my life. My heart was filled with wild hope for my future.

 *Chapter 4*

Learning at an English Manor House

If we submit everything to reason our religion will be left with nothing mysterious or supernatural. If we offend the principles of reason our religion will be absurd and ridiculous . . . There are two equally dangerous extremes: to exclude reason, to admit nothing but reason.

BLAISE PASCAL

MORNING LIGHT POKED THROUGH MY sheer lilac curtains, picking out the dazzling colors of the stones on my jewelry box, which sat elegantly on my white dresser. The colored light seemed to dance on my wall, holding me in its spell. I yawned, lazily stretching as I lay back enjoying the rare luxury of a Saturday morning lie-in. I was contemplating our weekend away. It would be the first time that I would be at a church camp with the young people from Fairview. Little did I realize what lay ahead.

So it was on the morning of March 5, 1973, as we drove towards Oranjeville on the beautiful banks of the Vaal River, that Paul's and my courtship began. Warm sunlight was filtering through the trees as we walked hand in hand along the riverbank, and I felt as if God was smiling down on us. I was happy. I knew I was experiencing the delight of my first love, but I also had a sense that God had been deeply involved in our lives. He wasn't just sitting in heaven surrounded by angels singing; He was deeply involved in my plans and I knew that He was shaping my future.

Our pastor encouraged our relationship, as he sensed that we both had the call of God on our lives. We were inseparable, in love and passionate about Jesus. Our hearts were full of God dreams and what we could achieve together for His kingdom.

From an early age I sensed that God had a special purpose for my life. In one way I believe that everyone has a personal calling, a specific destiny to fulfill. But Paul and I felt that God was calling us to commit our lives completely to His service. We sensed that God had chosen us to carry out a specific and unique task for Him.

The call of God can appear mystical because it is so personal and this deep, internal sense is not easy to articulate. Martin Luther, the great fifteenth-century Reformer, said that God's call is heard by faith. For us, there was an innate sense that God was leading and guiding us into our future, and though we did not know where or how, we both knew it would require the kind of faith Luther was speaking of. Charles Spurgeon, the eloquent nineteenth-century British preacher, said that the call to ministry was an eagerness to do God's work. That adequately described the deep aspiration that was in our hearts.

To be honest, I did not understand how God could use an ordinary South African girl, but I wanted to be obedient to His calling on my life, and so I willingly surrendered to Him and asked Him to use me to advance His kingdom on earth.

It was the same with Paul. I fell in love with him the first time I saw him, but I was also attracted to him because of his passion and love for Jesus. I knew that God wanted to use us to make His world a better place.

We loved our pastor, and his preaching impacted both of our lives in a profound way. He was an Englishman and a great expositor. His teaching inspired us and our desire to serve God grew under his leadership.

He and his wife had come to lead the Fairview Assembly, but had only committed to staying for a year. Before they left to go back to the United

Kingdom, they gave us the address of the Bible college in England they had previously attended. Our pastor's parting words to us were, "Perhaps this college is where you should go and prepare yourselves for ministry." Our destiny was wrapped up in those few simple words as God began to unfold His plan for our lives.

August 5, 1974, was one of those blustery autumn days in Johannesburg where the buttery-colored powder from the mine dumps filled the air as the wind tossed it about. Paul's family and mine were at Jan Smuts International Airport to bid us farewell. When Dad drove our Chrysler out of the gates of our yellow-brick house, I did not know that I would never again sleep in my lilac bedroom or eat another meal around our kitchen table.

My heart was full of mixed emotion that day. I was excited that Paul and I had a destiny and a calling to serve God and His world, but I was sad to say good-bye to my family and friends. Conflicting emotions have often had to live side by side in my journey through life.

We stood in a big circle at the airport as Pastor Potgieter began to sing in his rich baritone voice, "Till we meet again . . . till we meet at Jesus feet." I tried to be brave, but as I stood there the tears coursed down my cheeks because I was leaving my beautiful, sun-drenched land.

My heart was sore as I thought of my parents. I would even miss the squabbles and disagreement with my siblings.

Good-byes are never easy, but what I didn't realize then was that this was the first of many other good-byes that would become one of the patterns in the rhythm of our lives.

Through the years the farewells from loved ones have never got any easier, but we have willingly accepted God's call on our lives and the adventure and cost—those seemingly incongruent components—that come with it.

We arrived at Mattersey Hall Christian College in Mattersey, England, on September 17, 1974. An imposing red-brick manor house stood prominently in the center of the grounds. We entered a beautiful wood-paneled room filled with faculty and students.

I was apprehensive and a little overwhelmed, but before long we were welcomed and made to feel at home. Off to one side of the room was a young girl approximately my age. I knew from her accent that she was not British. I still remember her short bobbed hairstyle, tartan mini skirt, bobby socks, and tennis shoes. I liked her the minute I saw her. Her name was Joanna.

We were assigned our rooms. Mine was the large one on the top floor, right next door to Mr. Powell, none other than the college president. Of all the rooms on that landing, I had to be assigned the one next to the imposing leader of the college. How utterly unfortunate and incredibly scary! I would not feel free to put a foot out of place.

My room was so large that it could house at least eight girls, but initially there were only four occupants. It was a dull space and wore the look of countless years of neglect and decay. There was a huge bay window that allowed dappled shafts of light in when the sun managed, rather infrequently, to push through the clouds. There was also a window seat framing an old and inefficient heating system that overlooked the front lawn and some imposing hundred-year-old trees. But despite the evidence of a severe shortage of funds—the threadbare carpet, the fading paint, and the many indentations in my mattress where numerous other bodies had lain before—it became my new home and I loved it.

I was unpacking my belongings, settling into my room, and tucking my suitcase under the bed when suddenly the door burst open and in barged the girl with the tartan mini skirt. "Hello, my name is Joanna. I am from Waco, Texas." I knew I was right; she certainly did not have an English accent. We connected immediately.

Joanna's parents were missionaries in Afghanistan, and she had come to college chiefly because her parents wanted her there. She did not realize yet that God also wanted her there and He had a plan for her life. Over the next few years Joanna would grow into a wonderful and godly woman.

One of the first things I had to do when I arrived at college was report to the matron. She had crimson-red cheeks and a round, happy face with a beaming smile, which made her joy contagious. She handed me a roster and told me to fill in which night of the week I wanted to take my bath. I thought she was joking and nearly collapsed into giggles. But I was in a strange, new place, so I contained my urge to laugh and instead bit my tongue to keep from blurting out, "I bath every night." I was encountering my first bit of culture shock.

Of course, this was many years ago, and Britain was still trying to regain their footing after the tumultuous years of war. The Second World War caused unprecedented hardship and suffering, and when we arrived in England the country was still in the process of recovering from those bleak years. Politically the government was left leaning, and there was a pervasive sense of financial restraint in the nation.

Unemployment was at a high level, and the labor unrest that would later emerge in violent mine workers strikes was already festering. Council housing was touted as the solution to the growing population, replacing homes lost in the war. They were bleak; dismal places with row upon row of small, grim houses all mimicking each other.

This was a stark contrast to the wide-open spaces I had left in beautiful South Africa. The economy in England was weak, and so purse strings were tight. Many people could not afford the luxury of bathing every night because electricity and water were costly. The college had gone through some lean years as well, and there were obviously tight budget restraints. For a South African girl, this was a challenge second to none. The 1960s and '70s were boom years in South Africa, and I had not known any kind of deprivation growing up. I relished every one of the privileges afforded me; I bathed when I wanted, ate what I liked, and had all the necessities of life in abundance.

Still, where there is a will there is a way, and so I managed to find a circuitous route around this little problem of the restrictive bathing roster. At the end of one of the long corridors on the top floor was a bathroom that was used exclusively by senior students. It had a shower, which was the only one in the entire manor house. I figured that a short daily shower was equal to a long, luxurious weekly bath.

Undeniably I was breaking a college rule every single day, but I managed to justify my decision by reminding myself that "Cleanliness is next to godliness." I would willingly break the rules to be clean and godly.

(Here's hoping that a copy of this book never finds its way into the matron's hands. If it does, I trust she will pardon my iniquity and naivety and find it in her heart to forgive me. Although that is probably not the only thing she would need to pardon me for. But confession time is now over!)

If I wasn't with Paul, I was with Joanna. We became firm friends over the next few years. One Sunday, early on, we were playing badminton on the lawn outside the manor house. We were enjoying our game and becoming increasingly animated as it progressed.

Suddenly we heard a scurry of footsteps and a very stern looking dean of students appeared on the lawn. Anger was etched on his face as he stormed up to us, demanding that we stop our game immediately. With his gaze firmly fixed on the two of us he bellowed, "How can you dishonor the Lord in such a way?"

I was stunned and swallowed hard. "Is playing badminton a sin in England?" I mumbled.

He looked with strange bewilderment at this ignorant South African girl and her American friend. He paused, considering my foolish question, and then told us in no uncertain terms that, "Playing badminton on a Sunday is totally forbidden." In fact, there was very little that we were permitted to do on a Sunday. It was supposed to be a day of rest, and apart from going to church and eating, most other enjoyments were forbidden. Here was another culture shock.

I was devastated when I found out that we could not buy ice cream on a Sunday. Going to the corner shop and buying a frozen treat on a Sunday had been a family, as well as a church, tradition in South Africa. After church, all the young people from Fairview piled into cars and went to buy a vanilla ice cream cone dipped in hot chocolate. Now I felt utterly deprived of my Sunday delicacy.

I am pleased to say that now, forty years on, the legalism I was subjected to has by and large been dispelled from the churches to which I related.

It can be disorienting when you are in a new place surrounded by different people and subject to strange, new experiences. When people do and say things that are outside the realm of your current reality and their values are incongruent with yours, you begin to wonder if there is something wrong with you.

At times I felt frustration brewing away quietly inside of me; I only hoped it wouldn't erupt in some unbecoming way. As perfect as my country and her worthy inhabitants appeared from my perspective, I knew it had its fair share of stubborn, hardheaded, and difficult people and that many of their values were anything but perfect.

England had traditions and cultures that were different to mine, so I needed to make the necessary adjustments to fit into my adopted country. It was not my place to impose; I had to make the changes. I was learning to value the other, and I was also gaining a respect for people who were unlike me. These would be lifelong lessons that God would instill in me and would help me apply in the future.

I imagine that for Peter the apostle, this journeying into a foreign culture was a similarly disorienting adventure. In order for the Lord to use him in reaching the Gentiles, he had to go through some disconcerting and uncomfortable experiences. Like Peter, I needed the blinders of my culture to be removed so that I could see others from God's perspective.

There were other adjustments I had to make. I had come from the southern hemisphere, so I was not used to the grey skies and perpetual rain. The cold seemed to creep into my bones so that I was never warm. I would lie in bed at night with the door tightly closed watching the curtains on the windows billowing as the wind howled in through every corner and crevice of the old manor house.

I found the food stodgy and bland, and we ate copious amounts of potatoes cooked in every conceivable way. I am pleased to say that English cooking has progressed and there is now an abundance of fine and flavorful food.

I remember some of the men students coming to the girls one day with a story that seemed far-fetched. To this day they stand firmly by their story.

They were on kitchen duty, which meant that they would be up to their armpits in dirty dishes. Their added task on this particular day was to give the deep fryer its monthly clean.

The old oil was drained from the fryer and the students had to soak it in suds and then scrub it clean before it went back to the arduous task of frying potato after potato, day after day, week after week. That deep fryer was dearly beloved by every English student, for it ensured they would have their daily ration of fried potatoes.

On this day, when the particular student had discarded the grease and his hands were painstakingly scrubbing the large oblong pan, he felt something strange and hard at the bottom of the pan. Carefully he brought the specimen to the surface and upon examination discovered the skeleton of a rather large field mouse.

Imagine his joy in relaying the story to all the girls who despised rodents. Admittedly, I led the charge in detesting the pink-eyed, furry, lice-ridden little creatures. His sheer delight as we squealed and moaned at the thought of sharing our meals with a mouse was for him worth scrubbing his fingers to the bone.

Sharing a room with girls from other cultures stretched me, and I was learning to adapt and modify my attitudes and behavior. One particular morning, I was in chapel worshipping the Lord when one of my roommates quietly slipped into the service hoping to remain unnoticed because worship had already started.

As I caught sight of her, I noticed she was wearing a pale-lemon blouse with pretty, embroidered flowers on the sleeves. It looked exactly like the one I had purchased two days before, and I was amazed that she possessed one as well. She sat down abruptly next to me and I whispered; "Where did you get that blouse?" With a quizzical expression she muttered; "From your cupboard."

This was one of those occasional moments when I was completely lost for words.

As I sat there, I instantly felt flames of anger ignite inside of me. The words of the speaker drifted over the top of my head as my spirit festered with fury. *How could she help herself to my personal belongings?* I thought.

All through the service I contemplated my words and determined to give her a piece of my mind. I had no idea what the preacher preached that morning because I was far too engaged with my thoughts.

The moment chapel ended I accosted her with my words. Lashing out, I said, "How dare you invade my privacy and help yourself to my clothes?"

She looked at me, embarrassment creeping across her face as the color rose in her cheeks. "Sorry, I thought you wouldn't mind . . . I hoped . . . we were good enough friends." She stumbled over her words, close to tears. And with that she went hastily down the long corridor to avoid a further deluge of rage.

It is strange how quickly emotions can shift. One moment you can be filled with anger, and the next instant you are overwhelmed with remorse. Suddenly, shame for my harsh words and selfish heart washed over me like waves, and, just as quickly, the flame of anger I had nurtured during chapel was extinguished. I felt sorry and humbled. I had prayed that God would change others, but He was gently showing me that I was the one who needed to do the changing. This was a humbling but growing time in my life.

I enjoyed most of the lectures, but honestly, some were too long, others were incredibly boring, and a couple of them were above my intellectual capacity, going right over the top of my head. However, I was hungry to learn, and I had an appetite for God's Word. And so, even when a lecturer droned on in his monotone voice, I would be looking for the small nugget of truth that could nourish me and help me to grow.

I opened my heart to God and asked Him to look into every corner and crevice and weed out anything that could hinder my spiritual growth and love for Him. I welcomed Him to reign in my heart and to use me in any way He chose. I learned to adapt to the culture of my adopted country and accept the things I could not change. God was opening my eyes to see people from His perspective, and my cross-cultural conversion was preparing me to serve His world and become a global Christian.

Paul and I also quickly volunteered for various ministry opportunities. We started a children's club in the village where the college was situated. We seized every opportunity to travel with ministry teams. It was not long before we were both preaching in churches up and down the nation. We learned the valuable lesson of being available to serve God whenever an opportunity arose. These experiences and lessons helped forge the values and choices that have characterized our lives in Christian leadership.

As we were coming to the end of our time at Mattersey, we began to pray about our future and what God wanted us to do for Him. We had maintained our friendship with our pastor from Fairview, who was now living back in the UK. We spent meaningful hours with him and his wife, and they made a lasting investment in our lives.

One night as we sat in their cozy home, gathered around a beautiful log fire, Paul opened his heart and spoke about our desire to be used by Jesus. Our pastor responded with enthusiasm, saying, "Start a journey of faith."

I sat staring intently at him and thought, "What does he mean?" But at the same time I was filled with anticipation at the thought of an adventure of total dependence upon God.

Our pastor offered to help open a door for us to work at Teen Challenge in New York City for a number of months, and then encouraged us to anticipate that God would continue to open doors for us. It sounded scary. Little did we realize that God's will for our lives was once again wrapped up in the words of our pastor. We had no idea where all of this adventure was heading, but our hearts were full of wild hope.

On July 10, 1976, one of the hottest summer days in twenty years, Paul and I were married in the little village of Mattersey. My parents and siblings came over from South Africa to celebrate the occasion with us. We were married in a twelfth-century Norman church, nestled in the heart of the village.

As the sun broke freely through a sky filled with the fragrances of summer, people from all over gathered to celebrate the occasion with us.

Joanna and my two sisters were my bridesmaids. My brother and Paul's best friend, Ian Green, were Paul's groomsmen.

The ancient trees in the garden of the old manor house, clothed in evergreen foliage, lined the gravel driveway, their huge boughs meeting the branches on the opposite side to form a dark, leafy tunnel. A horse and a cart carried me down the narrow path from the manor house through the village to the church.

The streets were filled with a joyous atmosphere as the villagers gathered to catch a glimpse of the wedding party on this glorious summer day.

I entered the huge, arched doorway of the stone church. The walls were thick, but the windows were narrow and only allowed minimal light to shine through; this gave the church a somewhat somber and austere appearance.

I walked nervously down the seemingly endless aisle, smiling, happy faces greeting me from both sides. Family and friends gathered together in the nave, watching as we stood at the altar exchanging vows with each other.

Standing next to Paul that day, I remembered those words God had spoken to me in the quiet of the night. I was filled with gratitude and love.

We pitched a beautiful marquee tent on the front lawn of the manor house and had a South African *braaivleis* (a South African term for meat cooked over open, hot coals) to rival all others. It was a special day—the beginning of our lives and ministry together.

We were filled with wild hope and expectation for our future together.

Leaving the beautiful twelfth-century Norman Church after our marriage ceremony on July 10. 1976.

Reflection

I have always believed that life is one long adventure. Even in the midst of challenging times I have ensured that no experience is ever wasted. I think we can learn from every situation we encounter, and I have always tried to be a lifelong learner. If you are facing a particular challenge, ask God to help you to learn the lesson He is trying to teach you through this experience.

Paul and I have surrounded ourselves with people who give us honest counsel and advice. I am grateful for the way God has used upright men and women to help us learn, as well as find direction and leading. I see our lives as a puzzle, and bit by bit the pieces are placed into position so that the picture God has in mind will be complete and perfect.

I stand in awe at the way God has used friends, peers, and leaders to help position us for the next phase of our lives and ministry. The older we get, the more we rely on our friendships, and they are often our best sounding boards in times of uncertainty. Don't try and do things on your own. Surround yourself with trusted friends, your church community, and trusted leaders that can help you through difficult moments.

Through the journey of life, I have discovered how important it is that our hearts remain soft and pliable so that the Lord can mold us into vessels fit for His plan. In the midst of the difficulties and challenges of living in another culture, God was shaping me and giving me a worldview and perspective that was His. I realize there is no right or wrong culture—there are only different cultures. I certainly needed this perspective as God readied us for the next chapter of our lives.

Whatever situation you may be facing, let me assure you God is there. God remains the same whether you feel Him or not. Your circumstances may seem over-whelming, but allow God to take your hand and walk with you through this season. Open your heart to learn from Him. Surround yourself with trusted friends and allow your heart to be filled with His wild hope.

We drove back to our wedding reception at the old manor house in a quaint horse and trap.

Chapter 5

Faith Grows at Clinton Avenue

To one who has faith, no explanation is necessary.
To one without faith, no explanation is possible.

THOMAS AQUINAS

WE LEFT ENGLAND WITH SEVENTY-FIVE dollars in our pockets, and nearly all of those precious dollars were consumed by our first taxi fare in the US. We landed at JFK airport in New York late at night. Wind was throwing cold sheets of rain from the sky with the dismal threat that winter was on the doorstep and would not be kept at bay for much longer. Both of us sat quietly in the cab as we drove through the neon-lit streets of New York. Excitement and awe, mingled with sheer exhaustion, rendered us speechless as we made our way through the bustling city.

We arrived at Teen Challenge in Brooklyn, New York, on a chilly fall night, full of anticipation and excitement. In his deep nasally accent, our cab driver informed us that Brooklyn and the Bronx were two of the most unsavory boroughs of New York. With emphasis, he told us that he had every intention of preserving his life for a few more years, which meant that he was staying in his cab while we got our own bags out the trunk. And that was our welcome to Brooklyn!

We were young and ready for the adventure ahead; nothing could thwart our enthusiasm. Our pastor from England had written ahead to the director of Teen Challenge and recommended that we work at their New York center for three months. We were ecstatic when the opportunity opened for us to assist with rehabilitating drug addicts and teaching them the Bible.

We exited the cab onto a street littered with shattered glass bottles, trash, and the stench of urine. Homeless people, wrapped in newspaper and plastic bags to protect themselves against the elements, drifted aimlessly down the street.

We rang the doorbell of one of the Teen Challenge apartments and were quickly ushered in off the street, given a friendly welcome, and then shown to our little apartment. The walls were the color of green apples, and there was a semblance of orderliness even if the atmosphere was a little stark. We had two suitcases, empty pockets, and each other. In worldly terms, we were poor, but in every other way we felt rich.

A cacophony of noise filled the air as we laid our heads to rest that night. Sounds of dogs barking, horns honking, and the high-pitched screech of a woman in the apartment across the road from us stretched on into the dark. The night was alive with the constant *whoop whoop* of police sirens, but eventually sleep prevailed as our eyes closed and the sounds of Brooklyn faded.

We got involved in teaching the Bible to the men at the center. Many of their stories moved us deeply. It is easy to regard drug addicts in a rather stereotypical way, but beneath the surface one often finds dysfunctional and deeply hurt souls—the slippery slope to drink and drugs is often the consequence of their pain and loneliness. Unless we have walked in their shoes and lived their story, what right do we have to judge them? If we are willing to get alongside the helpless, the downtrodden, and the hurting, we have the right to an opinion, but until then the legitimate response is compassion.

We ran a weekly Kids Club in the neighborhood. I remember the deep sense of sadness I felt for the children. Most of them had shabby clothing, and only a few were fortunate enough to have shoes to cover their calloused feet. Many of their parents lived for one thing: the next fix. Their priority was not to feed their children and fill their bellies with food, it was to infuse their veins with heroin. As the white liquid entered their veins, a quick euphoric rush would banish the gnawing pain inside of them and still their trembling limbs, only to return with a vengeance once the white substance wore off.

Some mothers so desperate for the next dose would sell their bodies for a few dollars to any man who would have them. Men would take food from their children's plates just to ensure another euphoric rush. Despair and sadness filled their homes as their lingering habit emptied them of their dignity and self worth. Hope was gone, dreams shattered, and misery their daily lot.

Anguish, compassion, and frustration welled up inside of me as I saw the plight of these children. I suppose these feelings are what make us human. But the human capacity to hold different emotions in tension is what makes us unique. The result of these feelings always produces some kind of reaction from us. One response is to get involved in the lives of the poor and needy in compassionate ways. I believe this should be the reaction of every Christ follower.

Unfortunately, some Christians buy into the individualistic and self-serving philosophy of our society and turn a blind eye to the plight of the downtrodden and outcast. Sometimes we are consumed with our own lives and we don't want to get our hands dirty. However, I think another response is far more dangerous and can actually corrupt the soul of a Christian, and that is when we become hardhearted and judgmental, which produces a pharisaical response. In other words, we turn our heads the other way and with a sigh of relief thank God we are not like those sinners.

Paul and I knew we would only be at Teen Challenge for three months, and we felt desperation at not being able to disciple these children in their faith. The death and resurrection of Jesus motivated and inspired us to take His message to these precious little ones. We longed to see their world infused with wild hope. We wanted to pick up the broken fragments of their lives and fill their world with optimism—help them to rewrite their stories with Jesus in the center. Many of them started to recast the narrative of their lives, and our deepest prayer was that God would enable them to live out their newfound story in the midst of their broken and dysfunctional homes.

We were living by faith and had no money for necessities, but we determined to talk only to God about our needs. As an example, I was thankful I had brought the small tube of toothpaste that we got on the plane on our way over to New York. It might sound strange to say, but that little tube was an example of how we trusted God to provide for us.

It dawned on me that that little container of toothpaste, which generally only lasts a couple of uses, only emptied out when a gift of money was anonymously slipped under our door and we were able to go and buy our first tube of toothpaste as a married couple. Only God could make a tiny tube of toothpaste last for almost three months when two people were brushing their teeth twice a day—a miracle indeed!

As the weather began to turn, the bitter cold and biting wind simultaneously ushered in the snow.

By early December, snow had blanketed the city in white, and the temperatures plummeted well below freezing. When the temperature rose slightly, beautiful white flakes would freeze, go crunchy, and then turn to grey slush. This squelchy liquid would seep into our shoes, turning our feet to popsicles. I was never more miserable than when my feet felt like blocks of ice.

Paul grew increasingly concerned at my lack of warm winter clothing. He was far more anxious about me than I was about myself. He poured out his heart to God at breakfast one morning and asked the Lord to provide money to purchase a coat and a pair of boots for me. Within a few hours of praying, God did what he had asked, and an anonymous gift was slipped under our apartment door with exactly enough money for a warm coat and fleece-lined boots. We were thankful!

As our time at Teen Challenge drew to an end, we prayed about our next step. We began to get invitations to speak in churches and quickly realized that we would need a car if we were going to be traveling from church to church. So we prayed for money for a car. We had no income because we were serving on a voluntary basis at Teen Challenge, so we prayed about every need; it was the most wonderful time of our lives. Our faithful, heavenly Father cared for us in the most tender and loving ways.

A trendy church in downtown Manhattan invited us to do services for them. It was a unique church, and many celebrities would slip into the service and listen to the singing and preaching. We felt honored and privileged at the opportunity to preach there.

Our week there was wonderful, and after our final service the pastor came and thanked us for our ministry and handed us an envelope. You have to show incredible restraint in moments like that because your natural instinct is to tear open the envelope and see what is inside! When you live by faith you're anxious to know if God has provided for your need through an offering.

Paul suddenly felt an urge to go to the bathroom. He quickly excused himself and went and locked himself in the cubicle, where he ripped the seal open to see what was inside the envelope. There was two hundred and fifty dollars. He was ecstatic; this would be more than enough money to buy our first car.

He sprayed the air with praise, hoping that no one heard the jubilant sounds emanating from the little cubicle. A smile like a sunrise spread across his face as he exited the bathroom, and the twinkle in his eyes assured me that our need had been adequately met.

We returned to Teen Challenge elated by our week away and the generous provision of God. We shared our miracle with a number of the young men from the center. Some of them were skeptics, and they quickly snuffed out the flame of enthusiasm that had been ignited by the generous gift. I don't think they intentionally set out to discourage us, but I remember one young man collapsing in a heap of laughter as he bellowed, "Are you kidding? Two hundred and fifty dollars won't buy you a bicycle in New York!"

Unfortunately, that turned out to be pretty much true.

The following Sunday we planned to take the Teen Challenge minivan, with a number of the young men from the center, to one of the great inner-city churches of New York. Paul and I felt despondent about still not having any transport to fulfill the invitations to preach in other churches. As we were leaving for church that morning, Paul, the eternal optimist, uncharacteristically said to me, "Well, if God doesn't provide transport for us, how can we possibly accept all the preaching engagements we are getting?" I agreed with him and responded that getting around on a bicycle was not an option.

We arrived at the church and moved quickly and quietly to the balcony, as the service was ready to begin. The preacher, filled with enthusiasm, moved energetically from one end of the platform to the other, preaching with great gusto. And then, suddenly, he stopped in mid-stride, looked straight up into the balcony, and pointed his long index finger at the two of us.

I felt as if his eyes were penetrating my soul as he bellowed; "Don't you dare say you won't be able to serve God if He doesn't give you a car."

Our eyes rounded.

"Listen," he continued, "when God calls you, you say yes, even if it means getting around on a bicycle. Nothing and no one should stop you from serving God."

We were astonished! How on earth did he know what we had said in the privacy of our apartment? He didn't know, of course, but God did, and God used the preacher that morning to challenge our hearts. Or perhaps it was more than a mere challenge—it was conviction.

Guilt and conviction are two different emotions. In my view, guilt is a negative emotion that can produce feelings of remorse and despondency, which can lead to despair. Guilt generally does not produce positive change. Satan often uses guilt to inhibit us and make us falter in our walk with the Lord.

Conviction, on the other hand, is a positive emotion, which the Holy Spirit uses to prompt change in our lives. When we respond to conviction, there are always positive outcomes.

We got back to our apartment, knelt beside our bed, committed ourselves to Jesus wholeheartedly, and told Him we would go anywhere, anyhow, anytime—car or no car.

A few days later, we caught a bus to the Teen Challenge center in Rehrersburg, Pennsylvania, where we had accepted an invitation to teach for a two-week period. We had hoped to drive a car, but we hadn't been able to purchase one with the two hundred and fifty dollars we had been given, so we caught a bus. We stayed with a delightful young couple in their cozy little trailer. Paul and I found American people so warm, hospitable, and generous, and everywhere we went we were treated with kindness.

Some friends told us that there was a gas station on Main Street where the owner was selling some cars. The day was a particularly bleak one; the sky was grey, and storm clouds brewed on the horizon. The ground was covered in deep snow, and the wind seemed to delight in picking it up and tossing it into the air.

With the cold powder still on our faces, we dusted off our boots and entered the gas station and enquired if the owner had any cars for sale. He pointed outside to one that was covered in snow; we couldn't even tell what color it was because it was completely concealed beneath copious layers of white flurries.

With his bare hands, Paul removed the ice-cold snow and uncovered a car the color of pale-green tomatoes. It was a 1962 Chrysler, with a V8 engine, massive fins on the back, and push buttons for gears. I thought it was the ugliest vehicle I had ever seen. Paul thought it was magnificent.

The owner handed us the keys and said, "If it starts, it is a good car because it has been under the snow for a couple of months." Paul got in behind the steering wheel, and as he turned the key, the engine roared to life.

He went straight inside and negotiated a deal with the owner. Our pale-green car, including insurance, cost us two hundred and fifty dollars—the exact amount the Lord had provided.

I can still feel the thrill of excitement that ran through me that moment. When God saw our willingness to serve Him, no matter what the cost, He graciously presented a vehicle to us.

It was the most hideous-looking thing I had ever driven, but Paul loved it, and God had provided it, so I humbly accepted it. It was a great car, which took us right across the United States, covering more than five thousand miles.

(A little addendum that is worthy of mention: when we left the US some eighteen months later, we sold our pale-green car for three hundred and fifty dollars.)

We were traveling all across the United States and Canada preaching in churches, school assemblies, ladies meetings, and anywhere a door opened. It was the most wonderful, stretching, growth period of our lives. We learned to be thankful for every small blessing that came our way.

As the days accumulated, so too did the layers of gratitude as we experienced God's incredible hand of provision in our lives. I suppose that is why, even to this day, thankfulness is an innate response of our hearts. We find ourselves whispering thank yous throughout the day as we experience the continued faithfulness of our God.

One day (prior to our gratitude phase), Paul was complaining about how much gas our car used. He grumbled, "We are only getting twelve miles to the gallon."

That meant little to me, but I suggested we should lay hands on the car and pray for it. At this point, I think he seriously wondered about the mental state of his new bride. But we were recently married, so he lovingly responded, "Okay, darling, you pray."

I launched into a conversation with Jesus, telling him how much money we were spending on gas (I should have known He was fully aware of that fact) and imploring Him to "heal our car." A simple prayer from a faith-filled heart! My journal records that "from that moment our car got seventeen miles to every gallon." The book of James 5:16 does say, "The prayer of a righteous person is powerful and effective."

An unexpected invitation to preach at a church in Wilkesburgh, Pennsylvania, came out of the blue. Instantly we felt a connection with the pastor and his wife. They had kindred spirits, and we had a wonderful week with them.

The weather was bitterly cold and we felt the chill penetrating our bones. Neither of us possessed a scarf or a pair of gloves, so we prayed that the Lord would provide for us. Before the evening service we went to the pastor's office, and there on his desk were two beautifully wrapped parcels. One said "To Paul, from Jesus" and the other said "To Carol, from Jesus." Yes, inside those two parcels were fleece-lined leather gloves and beautiful woolen scarves. I was overwhelmed by God's provision and His love and care.

We went from Pennsylvania to preach in a small church in Saint Paul, Minnesota. Paul and I were kindly hosted by a large family in their little home. Spring was endeavoring to push winter aside, but the cold outside made you feel that winter was winning the battle.

As the sun attempted to squeeze through the sky, dappled shades of rosy pink and lilac filtered through the barren branches of the trees. It appeared as if God had a giant paintbrush in His hand and was splashing the sky with color.

I sat quietly in the warm glow, sensing God was there. I did not hear an audible voice, but I felt His presence. And I felt God say, *"Trust me for everything, small and big. In time, you will have to trust me for millions of dollars."* I sat still, not wanting to disturb the sense of God's peace. How could I have known then exactly what those words meant? From this perspective in time, those words make sense, but back then I was a young girl desperate for God to use my life. I felt overwhelmed. But yes, that was a formative experience in my life, a defining moment that laid a foundation for our future, and an experience to draw strength from when we did not know where money would come from.

The chapters that follow will unravel the story of how God's plan unfolded and how we learned to trust Him beyond our wildest hopes and dreams. Neither of us could imagine the amazing adventures God had in store for us or the millions of dollars we would trust Him for in the future.

As I look back, I realize that the call of God and our love for His world are the forces that propelled us to do what we did. I have three journals packed with stories of God's amazing provision. But those stories are for another book some other time. Suffice it to say Paul and I learned faith at Clinton Avenue. From there, God took us to many different nations, and we preached in many places as God opened some of the most amazing doors. We went from the US to Canada and then on to Hawaii, Samoa, Fiji, New Zealand, and Australia. We eventually went back to South Africa for Christmas and then on to Israel, Greece, and Scotland, where we had New Year services.

We were excited as God was beginning to open the next chapter of our lives. Little did we realize what that chapter held for the two of us. In some ways, I am glad we cannot see into the future. It safeguards our soul from worry and also from pride.

Reflection

To be in God's will is the safest place. When we launched out in faith, we did not know what the future would be. None of us have any idea of what tomorrow holds—we only have this moment right here, right now. But we can have confidence in the God who holds our future.

You either trust God 100 percent or you don't trust Him at all. You cannot trust God a little. The Bible says in Proverbs 3:5, "Trust in the Lord with all your heart / and lean not on your own understanding." The biggest battle we face is the one with our minds. We want to trust God, but our thoughts keep getting in the way. Too often we try to rationalize and figure out how God will do things.

Trust is that simple childlike ability to believe God. A child believes implicitly that his Dad will catch him when he says, "Jump into my arms." When the child takes that leap, it is one of complete trust.

This is not a call to foolish or irresponsible behavior, but to a place of trust in a God who has proved Himself over centuries—a God who never changes and is the same yesterday, today, and into the future. This amazing God can fill your heart with a wild hope for today and tomorrow.

I needed this kind of trust and hope for the next season of life.

 *Chapter 6*

Strengthened Resolve at Farmview Road

We are always on the anvil; by trials God is shaping us for higher things.

HENRY WARD BEECHER

EXCITEMENT, MINGLED WITH APPREHENSION, FILLED our hearts, because a door had opened for us in the UK where a senior pastor had invited us to fill his shoes as he traveled to the United States. We were full of anticipation, but at the same time we were overwhelmed at the responsibility of filling this larger-than-life pastor's shoes when we were still so young and inexperienced. Encouraged by the news that there was a lovely, comfortable home for us to live in and that the six-hundred-member church was eager to welcome us, we bade farewell to Scotland and headed down south to lead this church in England.

We were young, energetic and passionate. Both of us felt honored and humbled that this door had opened for us with the opportunity to develop our preaching and leadership skills in this church. We had also recently discovered that we were expecting our first baby, and we were both elated.

We quickly found out that things at the church were not as promised. The truth was that we had to share the small house with the senior pastor, who had suddenly decided he did not want to travel to the US after all. I was expected to do his washing, ironing, cleaning, and cooking.

Paul discovered that he was not invited to the church to preach and develop his leadership skills, but rather he was expected to clean toilets, vacuum carpets, and run errands to and from the church. We didn't have a problem with working, cleaning, and getting our hands dirty, but we also wanted to minister and live out our calling in other tangible ways. We simply wanted to do what we had been invited to do. To say that our time was difficult and trying would not be an exaggeration.

On June 22, 1978, a strawberry-blonde, green-eyed baby girl entered the world and our hearts were smitten from the moment we laid our eyes on her. Her life colored a challenging and difficult year with joy. We called her Anna, which means, "one of grace"—a fitting name for someone who would exhibit this characteristic throughout her lifetime.

On the second day after Anna's birth, the senior pastor informed Paul that he was not allowed to visit me in the hospital. He said it was unnecessary to be visiting a wife and baby when there was work to be done in the church.

I was only twenty-one years old, living in a foreign country with no other family members around me. I felt alone.

I decided then and there that I would discharge myself from the hospital so that I could at least be in the familiar environment of my home. If my husband couldn't visit me, I wanted to be in my own surroundings and close to him.

Just prior to Anna's birth, we had been fortunate to have a kind and generous friend help us to purchase a little home on Farmview Road. It was there that we brought Anna to spend the first few months of her life. It was also in this little home that I would strengthen my resolve to be faithful to Jesus and His calling no matter what the cost. This was the first time in our married lives that we were living on our own and it felt wonderful to have a little place for the three of us.

The night after I returned home was the Saturday night prayer meeting at the church, and although I had only delivered Anna two days previously,

I was anxious to attend with Paul. After the meeting concluded the senior pastor summoned Paul and me into his office. I was surprised to see him sitting there with two of the elders of the church. We were shown two chairs and told to take a seat. The senior pastor then turned his attention toward me. With an elder on either side of him he drew himself to his full height and glared at me, telling me that I was cold hearted and I did not love people.

I was too stunned to say a word; I felt my vocal chords tighten in my throat. I had no idea why he thought I showed no love for people. Admittedly, I was shy, young, and inexperienced, but my love for people was the reason why I had sought a life in the ministry. How he came to such a conclusion left me bewildered and troubled. Perhaps I had been withdrawn, but then we had been given strict instructions from this man not to make friends with people in our congregation. With an order like that, I wondered how it was possible to show expressions of love and care for people.

Reflecting back, I recall how deeply hurtful his pronouncement was. Words are powerful, and his were like a knife piercing my soul. He then went on to tell me I was selfish. For this assumption, he at least gave me a reason. He said I expected my husband to spend time with our newborn baby and me when there were people who needed him to be available for their needs. I needed to learn what sacrifice was; I needed to learn to put the needs of others before my own. In his view, that meant letting go of my husband so that he could give himself 100 percent to God.

I took his verbal lashing quietly and submissively and did not say a word. I couldn't. I was stunned and hurt. My throat was taut, and I felt myself swallow hard to ensure those salty tears burning in the corner of my eyes did not surface.

I do recall that at that moment I resolved that if God ever permitted me to influence other young lives, I would treat them with honor and respect. I determined that if I ever needed to challenge or confront a young person, I would speak the truth in a loving way, as the Bible exhorts us to do.

Now I realize that this type of leadership was nothing less than controlling, manipulative, and abusive. I would never tolerate that abuse today, but it opened my eyes to everything a servant leader is never meant to be and everything I determined never to aspire to.

I am grateful for that difficult year, not because I enjoyed the hand that we were dealt, but because some deep, foundational lessons were layered into our lives at a defining time. And for that I thank God. I am amazed at how He can take brokenness and turn it to good. We resolved to be servant leaders who would never use manipulative tactics, never seek to control people or be abusive in any shape or form.

Eventually, an opportunity presented itself to return to South Africa and serve in a church there. Although our departure from England was not easy, neither of us could wait to leave the bleakness we had been subjected to. This is by no means a reflection on the church as a whole—there were many wonderful and godly people in that church who had loved us and shown us kindness even if the senior pastor had been brutal and unkind. It is simply a perspective on abusive leadership, which unfortunately occurs too often in too many places all over the world. The combination of the senior pastor's need to control and his innate skepticism were a potent mixture that displayed itself in the most toxic way.

To our surprise and delight, the elders informed us that they were taking up a love offering for us on our last evening. However, when they handed Paul the envelope there was no money inside, only an invoice informing Paul that he owed the elders his entire love offering. He was baffled and enquired as to the reason. They informed him that we had taken a two-week holiday to the States earlier in the year, and after re-evaluating the situation, they decided it should be unpaid leave. Hence, we owed the church seventy pounds.

The ominous and bleak weather that final evening seemed to mirror and reflect the gloom in our souls. Our car had already been sold, and so a kind friend from our church drove us to our almost empty home to pick up the last of our belongings. Paul sat quietly in the car; like a clay soldier, cold and stiff, he did not budge or make a sound.

We got back to the little home where we had spent the past year, gathered our few remaining belongings, and looked one last time around the empty, barren room.

Standing in the kitchen, peering into the darkness, we felt a wave of emotion suddenly wash over us as we reflected on the events of the past. As despondency rolled over us, all the injustices of a miserable year spilled out and we wept.

I wish we could wash our memory, erase from our minds the harsh and brutal verbal abuse, but can we ever really extinguish memories?

There are three things we *can* do with our memories. We can push them aside and never truly face them or deal with them. We can bury them deep in our psyches and trust that they won't resurface. Or we can courageously face our memories and deal with them. Although I wanted to scrub the memories from my mind, I realized how important it was to deal with our reality no matter how hurtful it had been.

It would have been easy to extract this story and leave it buried in the far corners of my mind and the pages of my journal. But that wouldn't have been right; in fact, it would have been disingenuous. If we tell our story, we have to be honest about the good and bad, the victories and defeats, and the joys and sorrows.

Sometimes life is tough. In his book *The End of Memory: Remembering Rightly in a Violent World*, Theologian Miroslav Volf coined the term "remembering rightly." In my view (and much of my thinking here is influenced by Volf), the ability to remember is a gift; the capacity to remember rightly is a discipline.

Over time, our memories can distort events of the past, and the perpetrators of our injustice can loom larger and more terrible than they actually were. Careful, deliberate, and honest reflection of past realities helps us to remember rightly, reminding us of our own personal flaws while at the same time seeking to look into the life of the perpetrators and understand their story and what caused them to do the things they did. This type of remembering is helpful for the soul because in reflecting on our own humanity and frailty we can see others in a whole new light.

Introspection can be helpful when we use it as a tool to become better people. As we look inside and acknowledge those areas of our lives that need to change, we can then equip ourselves to be more useful in the future. We would never appreciate the good times if we had never experienced difficulties. Sometimes it is the dark and difficult times that shape us the most. The sunshine of today is more glorious in the light of the dismal overcast day that just passed.

We are all imperfect humans, some more imperfect than others. The one lesson we must take from our pain is that we should do everything in our power to avoid causing others pain. If we do not learn this important lesson, our suffering is in vain. I have no regrets about this time in our ministry, and I quickly forgave anyone who hurt us. I would never change my calling for any other vocation, even though it has not been without its challenges.

After a year in the church, we left the shores of England for our beautiful, homeland, South Africa. We arrived home on a sun-splashed day in time for Christmas celebrations. I enjoyed being home with my family and felt re-energized by church and friends. I handed over my hurts to Jesus and was filled with renewed hope for our future. I didn't realize then how much I would need it for the next season of my life.

As I have lifted the veil and peered down the corridor of God's goodness, my eyes have welled up with tears and my heart has filled with gratitude. Our lives have been full of color in every season, and as the corner of the curtain of our youth turned, it revealed a new and different, but equally exhilarating, blaze of color—the color of wild hope.

Reflection

Reflecting over that period of our lives, I realize that no experience was wasted. I love the good and happy stories that make me feel all fuzzy and aglow, but I am also thankful for the valuable faith lessons I learned in the early days of our ministry. Somehow the not so good stories have also been an important and integral part of the puzzle of our lives.

It was in part those difficult and stretching times that made Paul and me the people we are today. Bitterness and anger have never been options. We have always sought to discipline our hearts from allowing the awful root of resentment to penetrate our souls. And I really do mean intentional discipline. When one of us has been tempted to say something unkind about someone that wronged us, the other one has quickly stepped in to halt that conversation from going further. We are both intent on God using us in His world, and we never want bitterness or any other negative emotion to hinder our effectiveness.

If you are hurting, I urge you to give that hurt to Jesus and allow Him to replace it with hope. Of course, that does not justify the harm that has been done to you, but what it does do is free you as a person so that the problem is no longer yours. Jesus will avenge you in His time. That does not mean that you deliberately seek revenge; it means that you trust your heavenly Father to do what is right and good for the other.

As I let go of my hurt and pain, Jesus replaced it with a newfound hope that would see me through the next season of my life. I can only describe it as wild hope!

 Chapter 7

God's Protection in the Loneliness of Aristata Avenue

The best cure for loneliness is developing an intimate relationship with Jesus Christ.

ANONYMOUS

THE YEAR WAS 1979. FIVE years previously, we had left home as two single young people. Now we were married, we were also parents, and we were seasoned travelers with layers of experience stored up inside of us and a good deal more wisdom than when our journey began. Exactly what we needed for the coming season of our lives.

A new day dawned, infusing us with vigor and joy at the promise of fresh opportunities. A church in Roodepoort, South Africa, had invited us as associate pastors. The senior pastor was an Irishman with a passion for life and God. Sam had married a South African girl, Louise, and together they opened their hearts, their home, and their church to us. We enjoyed every moment of our time in the church and we were given opportunities to grow and expand our leadership and preaching skills.

Sam and Louise were unthreatened leaders, and they encouraged and nurtured us in those early days of ministry. Every time Paul preached, Sam would feed him with encouragement. Paul soaked up the affirmation, and we both felt renewed passion and spiritual vitality simultaneously restored. We can sometimes think that affirmation makes us egotistical. Truth be told, we all need affirming, and as long as we receive and process it correctly, it can be beneficial to our soul. Paul had received harsh criticism from his previous leader, and to now have a mentor that endorsed and encouraged him was a balm to his soul.

We bought a pretty little house on 21 Aristata Avenue, Florida Glen. This home would become a sanctuary for the children and for me, and it would also be a place where I would learn many deep and meaningful lessons. I cooked hundreds of meals in my kitchen, bottled and stored copious amounts of apricot jam and peach preserves, and washed more diapers than I care to remember.

Yes, those were not the days of disposable diapers, and washing them required a number of steps to return the diaper to its previous state of dazzling whiteness. The first step was to rinse the diaper in the bathtub. Second, they were soaked in a special sanitizing solution for twelve hours. Once this process was completed, the diapers were thoroughly rinsed by hand. They were then carried off to the washing machine where they were boiled, washed, and rinsed for a third time. Finally, they were hung out to dry in the African sunshine.

On most sunny days, this could be as little as twenty to thirty minutes. When they were dry, they were taken off the washing line, folded, and packed away for further use.

Simple days, but happy!

I remember one particular Sunday evening when Paul was preaching. He was expounding a passage from one of the Gospels, explaining how God's mercy and justice displayed in Jesus could touch and heal broken lives. The silence was electric; you could hear a pin drop.

Suddenly the stillness was interrupted by a man's voice. He had been listening intently to every word spoken and appeared oblivious to anyone around him. It was almost as if he and Paul were alone in the sanctuary.

With intensity etched on his face and urgency dripping from his voice, he blurted out, "Are you telling me Jesus can make me whole, take away my pain, and give me a new life?"

Paul, sensing the urgency in the man's appeal and the sincerity with which he posed his question, attempted to answer him, but he was also acutely aware that four hundred people sitting in the sanctuary were eavesdropping on the conversation.

The man was fervent, almost desperate, the yearning in his soul palpable as he stood there unmindful of the many people around him. He was speaking to Paul, responding to the deep stirrings of God in his heart. As he continued in his own bubble, he asked Paul what he should do to become a Christ follower. Paul told the man that Jesus wanted a relationship with him and was waiting for him to make a decision. Then and there, the man prayed and invited Jesus to be Lord of his life.

I have been to many church meetings in my lifetime, but that one will always stand out because it was so unusual. The man lacked any kind of church etiquette. In fact, he had probably seldom been to church, if ever, and so he was unaware of church protocol.

I love it when people are stripped of religiosity. I wish we saw more authentic responses in our sometimes overly structured services. That man simply knew that he had heard a profound truth and he wanted Jesus to make him whole. It was a remarkable meeting and a sincere conversion.

About thirty years later, we were teaching our master of theology program in South Africa. A handsome young African man who had decided to do the graduate program came and introduced himself to Paul. He reached out his hand to Paul and said, "My father-in-law sends his greetings."

Paul was a bit baffled as to who the man's father-in-law was. He looked at the young African man, who was standing there with his beautiful little peaches-and-cream wife. And then he recalled the man who had given his life to Jesus in the service in Roodepoort. God's ways are majestic! Now, years later, this young relative of that man would study under Paul.

Jesus has a remarkable way of invading a life and sending it in a whole new direction. That gentleman's decision impacted his entire family and their futures in a deep and profound way. Now we witnessed the fruit of his decision. Suffice it to say, the young African man is an influential political leader in South Africa today and God's hand is on his life. We hope that he will influence our nation and be a voice in the midst of rampant secularism and relativism. We never know what fruit will come from the small seeds we plant.

During our time at Roodepoort I became pregnant again. It was shortly after hearing this wonderful news that Paul received his call-up papers for military service in the South African Border War.

War is terrible for many reasons, not least the loss of lives. But it can also wreak havoc in the lives of families. Just as our lives were gaining normality, his call threatened to disrupt the rhythm of our lives.

Life is often paradoxical. One side seems to be going smoothly while the other appears to spiral downwards. The challenge is how to handle the paradox and discipline ourselves to navigate contrasting experiences. I have found in those times I need to focus on the positive aspects of my life, not simply the things that are challenging. And that is not always easy.

We were enjoying the church at Roodepoort and were establishing new and wonderful friendships. The thought of being alone, with a toddler and a tiny baby, at a time in our lives and our nation's history when insecurity and war threatened our borders was alarming to me.

Paul had developed deep convictions about war and violence and had determined not to take up arms. As a result, he applied to serve in the chaplaincy, which would be a noncombatant role. He was relieved when he received this posting because he could still fulfill his calling and ministry while serving his country.

As my delivery date drew closer, we prayed that our baby would be born before Paul was due to leave for military service. His departure date was January 16, 1980. Early in the morning, on January 10, I woke up feeling a dull ache in my lower back and severe pressure in my abdomen.

I got out of bed and made myself a cup of tea and then ensured I had all my belongings packed and ready for an overnight in the hospital. At six a.m., we made our way to the hospital. At eight-twenty a.m. Jason

Paul Alexander took his first breath as the nurse seized his slippery form with both hands and welcomed him into the world with a thump on his posterior. He wasn't very impressed with her method of greeting and bellowed in response, assuring his mother and father that he had a perfectly good set of lungs.

He was a delightful addition to our family and his sister was thrilled to have a playmate.

January 16 dawned all too quickly; the intense summer sun streamed through our windows, rudely reminding us that the day we were both dreading had arrived. I can still see myself standing at the dining room window, broken hearted, waving good-bye to Paul. I used up all my tears on that day; I was sapped and emotionally drained.

Saying good-bye to family has become a part of the rhythm of our lives, but saying good-bye to each other is a struggle that has never diminished with time. I had to draw on all my inner resources to keep me focused on my babies and the positive aspects of my life in the midst of my profound loneliness and all too sudden state of singleness. Navigating the challenges of life and contrasting experiences was forged in the early days of ministry. And for that I am grateful.

I remember standing in the kitchen one day complaining to Jesus. "You called me to serve You, Jesus, and all I do is wash diapers and clean up the mess." Immediately, I heard God's gentle voice whisper to me. *"Enjoy these precious moments. Caring for your family is your ministry. This season will go by rapidly and the next one is at your heels."*

I needed to hear those words. I filed them carefully away in my brain for quick recall when necessary.

Raising my little girl and boy was the most important task for me, more important than the preaching and teaching that would constitute so much of my future. There have been so many times that I have longed to go back down the avenues of time and recapture some of those precious and sometimes far too hazy moments with my children. That is why it is so important to seize every second, enjoy each breath, and linger in the beauty of the moment. Time waits for no one.

If I could do it all over again, I'd lie barefoot on the grass with my little ones snuggled on each side and watch the sun creep behind the clouds. I would wait and see the sky turn into shades of peach and orange and allow its beauty to take my breath away. I'd linger until the stars were splashed all over the heavens and pause until their brilliance dazzled me. I would lie quietly, listening to my children breathing, and revel in the One who made them. I would marvel in His majesty and thank Him for another day to enjoy His creation.

Those moments are spent. My time with my children has come and gone. Maybe your time is now. Stop. Seize your moment, because before long you will be doing the reminiscing. I hope your reflections will be joyful ones.

Paul and I wrote to each other every single day. My letters were filled with copious details of Anna and Jay's antics, and my love for him spilled out and dried up many a pen. We lived for each other's letters.

A particularly trying time for Paul was when not one of my letters reached him for over six weeks. You can only imagine his despair as day by day every soldier received handfuls of mail, but he received none. Eventually the problem was sorted out and he received sixty-eight letters in one day. He read with hungry eyes as the letters detailed the events of our lives.

It was a growing and stretching time for me, which was not comfortable, but I learned to depend upon God. I talked to Him about every detail of our lives and understood what the Bible meant by God being a husband to the widow.

One of the greatest areas of concern was for Paul's safety. I never knew where he was stationed, and he could never reveal any of his whereabouts in his letters. Those were trying days in our nation's history.

Despite being a relatively advanced nation, television was only introduced to South Africa on January 5, 1976. This was chiefly because the country's white minority government under the National Party considered that its apartheid policies could be threatened if it lost control of the media. Initially, there was only one channel, but by 1981 we had two.

In spite of the lack of television, South Africans generally were well informed. Many were well read, and because they felt isolated from the world community, many had an insatiable appetite for information from around the globe. However in 1969, when everyone around the world sat glued to their television sets watching Neil Armstrong place his foot on the moon, South Africans could only listen to the dramatic event on the radio.

Initially, there were only a few hours of TV broadcasting in the day and a couple of hours at night. Every evening it was customary for SABC (South African Broadcasting Corporation) to scroll on television all the names of the men who had been killed in battle in the South African Border War. I prayed daily that I would never see Paul's name on the screen. These were anxious times, and yet precious moments too as I learned to trust the Lord in everything.

The South African Border War was a conflict that took place from 1966 to 1989 and occurred largely in South West Africa (now Namibia) and Angola. It was a war mainly between South Africa and its allied forces of the National Union for the Total Independence of Angola (UNITA) and the Angolan government on the one side, and the Southwest Africa People's Organization (SWAPO) and their allies (mainly Cuba) on the other.

Paul had the rank of colonel, which afforded him some privileges. One of those was the opportunity to phone home for a few minutes every couple of weeks. I lived for the phone calls, to hear his voice and know that he was still alive. We take little things for granted, but every phone call infused me with courage to face the challenges of another week. Hearing Paul's voice was music to my soul. He was alive! My heart would burst with gratitude.

Paul often shared some of the experiences he had while serving in Namibia, and I have to admit they kept me awake at night. He once recalled one of the more traumatic experiences he had. He was in the northern part of Namibia, which shares its borders with Angola and Zambia in the north, Botswana to the east, and South Africa to the south and east. Paul had determined not to take up arms, but in every other way he served alongside his men. He accompanied them unarmed into the bush with grenades and mortar bombs going off in every direction.

SWAPO had done a fair amount of damage in the area, and as a small truck laden with over twenty-two Ovambon people was heading back to their village, they drove directly over a landmine planted by SWAPO. The vehicle was blown to smithereens and only three young men survived. They were sitting on the tailgate and the blast sent them flying into trees some distance away. Paul helped to CASEVAC them to the helicopter before turning his attention to the nearly two dozen horribly mutilated bodies of the dead. He and the platoon doctor packed the bodies into body bags in order to return their gruesome remains to their relatives.

A few days later the bodies were placed in a little local church to await burial. The bodies lay in the building for over forty-eight hours as the blazing heat of the Ovambon sun penetrated the corrugated roof. Paul was asked to participate in the funeral for all the victims.

On the day of the funeral, the air was thick with humidity, and the smell of the rotting corpses hovered over the church like a noxious cloud. The heat was unrelenting and mingled with the inconsolable pain of the grieving families was an atmosphere of total despair.

War is a terrible thing! But in the midst of that tragedy, Paul had the opportunity to share about a God of peace and love who could touch and mend the broken-hearted, inviting them into a better tomorrow. As he shared about a God who understood their suffering, grieved with them, and walked beside them, the atmosphere filled with hope. Some of those desperate relatives became Christ followers on that tragic day. Even in war and the most devastating events, God is there, and He is present to comfort and to give hope.

Amidst all that horror, Paul had some amazing God interventions during his time in Namibia. Once, he was attending a commanding officers' conference, which required a two-hour journey in armed vehicles over dangerous roads. The group was in a hurry to begin the trip, and the engines on the vehicles were already running. Paul was not particularly popular when he insisted that the engines be cut and the men remove their headgear in order for him to pray. Having a senior rank, however, brought the appropriate response, and he was able to lead the men in prayer and asked specifically for God's safekeeping. As he said amen, a signals officer came running out to say that a plane was being sent for Paul and that the vehicles could follow on a little later.

Paul suggested that because of this delay, they have a meal at the base, but also requested that the minesweepers should go out and sweep the roads for mines in order to give the group a good start when they left. As they were having breakfast, another signal arrived saying that the plane had been canceled and that they should head off as soon as possible. Everyone climbed into the vehicles and once again Paul insisted on praying. This time, as he said amen, there was a loud explosion from less than a mile away. The detail was amazing.

Normally if the roads had not been swept for landmines, the vehicles would drive through the bush on the side of the road. On this particular day, one of the sweepers felt inclined to sweep the side of the road exactly where the vehicles would have been traveling that morning.

For some reason, this sweeper went into the rough terrain and found a landmine. The soldiers were astounded and declared from that moment they always wanted to travel with the chaplain. They recognized that his prayer had been answered. The delays as well as the unusual decision to sweep for landmines off the side of the road had resulted in their lives being spared.

I remember the feeling of loneliness that would creep over me at uncommon times. In the middle of a mundane activity, I would suddenly become aware that Paul was not there—that I could not share some of the joyful moments in the children's development with him.

Anna was walking and talking and Paul was not a part of this growth and developmental phase of her life. He was not seeing his little boy's first smile or first tooth, not watching him learning to crawl and say his first words—moments of time slipping away, never to be recaptured. My deepest sense of sadness to this day is all the moments Paul lost, and that our children were deprived of their daddy at such a fundamental stage in their lives.

I have two grandchildren now, and I want to cling to each second with them. I wish I could stop the clock from ticking and hold time in my grasp. I suppose that is why eternity will be special—because time will be locked up forever.

I was so busy being a single mom, doing laundry, cleaning, and washing diapers that I would often leave my children's questions hanging in the air while I rushed to answer the phone or complete a chore. I would silence their happy chatter for what now seem like rude and unwarranted interruptions.

Too late, I realized that there is nothing more important than focusing on each and every second with my two special God-given gifts. No call is so important that it cannot wait while you answer those silly, childlike questions and kiss their wounds.

When I look at my grandchildren and see their pure innocence, my natural inclination is to wrap them up in cotton wool and protect them. But I cannot do that. I can only pray that God will shelter them through the storms of life and safeguard their innocence while leading them into an uncertain future. But a future I believe and pray will be filled with a wild hope.

Reflection

Life is precious. It is a gift. Enjoy each moment. We have only this one before us now. Our past is gone and we should not live with regrets. We can be reflective and learn from our mistakes, but then we must move on and seize the present. None of us can be certain of tomorrow, so we must take life with both hands and live. Don't wish time away, but revel in the experience of the day. Breathe deeply and live passionately.

Life is challenging, and sometimes life throws things our way that we never planned for. That is why we are encouraged to put our trust in the Lord. He knows the end from the beginning and we can have complete confidence that He will order our steps. What can be more comforting than to know that the God that you place your trust in holds your future in His hands?

That in and of itself is a reason for wild hope—the kind that would permeate the next season of our lives.

I was ready for the next adventure to come our way; I had learned many important lessons. The most significant one was to place all my trust in the Lord. These lessons would hold me in good stead for the future and all that God had in store for us as a family.

I encourage you to let go of your past and place your trust in God for today!

 *Chapter 8*

God's Provision on Peebles Road

God's work done in God's way will
never lack God's supply.

JAMES HUDSON TAYLOR

PAUL FINALLY COMPLETED HIS MILITARY service and we received a call to go and lead our home church, Fairview Assembly of God. It was a prestigious church with a rich heritage. Paul and I had met at Fairview and it was there that our faith grew and from there we left to go to Bible college. Our invite to lead our home church was an honor.

The church had gone through a difficult patch, and our predecessor had taken half the members with him to pioneer a new church in another suburb. When we arrived at Fairview, it was diminished in size and the people who remained were discouraged. However, we love a challenge and so we worked hard, prayed much, and led the church in a new direction.

For me, going to Fairview was like going home. The church parsonage was only two blocks from my childhood home. It was wonderful to be back in my neighborhood with all the familiar places and people.

As humans, we often take comfort in the old and the familiar. The comfort that comes from the ticking sound of the old clock that has stood in the same place for years, or the weathered books on a familiar wooden shelf—they are simply material things, but they give one a sense of roots. That is how I felt when I arrived home. I belonged.

There is so much I could say about our years in Fairview, but the lasting impact of our time there was the amount of young people who went into full-time ministry as a result of our influence and encouragement. Today many of them are scattered across the world in Christian service. This season of ministry was fruitful and we both grew in our walk with the Lord.

One day, as the sun was bathing my kitchen with warmth and light and the fragrances of spring were filtering through my window, seeking to lure me outside, I resisted the urge as I stared at the huge pile of dishes in my kitchen sink. I stood scrubbing pots and pans, determined to get through my chores as quickly as possible so that I could enjoy the day. However, I must admit that tasks never seemed quite as arduous when I could look out the window and breathe in the intoxicating fragrance of the jasmine creeper climbing up the wooden pergola next to my kitchen wall.

I meditated on the Lord and thanked Him for His goodness and for settling us in Fairview. The church board had just completed an addition to the parsonage, giving Paul a spacious study and me a wonderful guest room for entertaining the many people that came our way. We felt secure and settled. I expressed my heartfelt gratitude to Jesus for bringing me home and for enabling me to put down roots in familiar soil. As women, much of our security comes from being entrenched in a community and letting our roots go deep.

After all the travel, I was grateful for the opportunity to return to my home and be nourished and sustained by my cultural and spiritual origins. I was also thankful for the opportunity to sow and invest back into the spiritual community where I had received so much encouragement as a young person.

Standing in my kitchen that day, I felt the warmth that comes from being secure and safe. I began pouring my heart out to Jesus for my children and thanking Him for helping us to get them into good schools.

I was alone with my thoughts floating through my mind like tumbleweed blowing through the fields on a windy day on the plains.

Suddenly, a car screeched up our front driveway and seconds later Paul burst through the backdoor of our home. He got a soapsuds hug, and then he led me down the passage insisting that he needed to tell me about an experience that he had just had. He was literally overwhelmed!

He had been sitting in his church office talking on the phone to a board member about some mundane business. The person ended the conversation by saying to Paul, "Well, things are going well and you are building a nice little nest for yourself." He then simply said, "Have a nice day!"

Paul put down the phone and these words resounded over in his mind and troubled him deeply. He fell on his knees and cried out to God, "The last reason why I breathe your air and am alive is to build a nice little nest for myself." It was in that moment that Paul had a profound and life-changing encounter with God.

He remembers his study flaming with light. He sat in electric silence as God's presence surrounded him in a tangible way. He could not utter a word as he sat hardly daring to breathe.

He is not sure how long he remained in that stillness and light, but suddenly the silence broke and God spoke three things clearly to him. The first thing was that we would leave pastoral ministry. Then God assured him that we would impact nations. And finally, that we would trust Him on behalf of others. This last statement was puzzling to Paul in the moment, but has made complete sense to us through the years since.

Paul's encounter with God on that day was so significant that he knew things would never again be the same. (And they have not been.) His immediate response to God that morning was, "Yes Lord, I will go anywhere and do anything that your will might require," and he jumped into his car and raced home.

"Darling," he exclaimed breathlessly as he steered me down the passage to a chair in our bedroom. "God is leading us into a new dimension of ministry." I met his gaze as his eyes lit up as if the blinds had just been opened and his face beamed with joy. I could sense he'd had a momentous experience. I knew within seconds of him speaking those few words to me that God was interrupting my life, cutting across my plans.

The church board had just completed the extension onto the parsonage and the church was undeniably growing by the week. My children were booked into good schools, and above all else, I was home and feeling that wonderful sense of belonging and security.

Hanging in the air like mist on a hazy day was one question: "How did this word from God fit with our lives?"

Quite simply, it did not, because His plans for our lives are grander and higher than our own.

God's plan did not fit with mine. The way I had conjured things up in my mind were no proof of God's seal of approval. Psalm 139:16, "All the days ordained for me were written in your book before one of them came to be." This verse has been a recurring scripture that has comforted me throughout the years. I have learned the place of quiet submission to His will for my life because I know His ways are best, even if I do not fully comprehend everything He is doing at a particular moment in time.

With complete peace I said to Paul, "I am ready for whatever God has planned for us."

Please don't think for one moment that changing the course of my life was easy and without its challenges. No! I faced the same struggles, the good-byes were just as difficult, and the sense of loneliness and trying to find my feet in a new place was at times overwhelming. However, I have learned that if Jesus goes before us and leads us in a new direction I can rest securely in Him. His will for our lives is the safest place on earth, even if that place is dangerous from a natural perspective. If He ordained my days before the world began, who am I to question Him?

Quite frankly, we did not know what the next step was. God had spoken, our hearts had responded yes, but what were we to do?

Paul is a pragmatist and so he suggested, "Let's take a road trip to White River and go and spend a few nights at Come Together guesthouse so that we can pray and reflect on what God is calling us to." I willingly agreed.

We packed our car and put our two little ones in their chairs on the backseat and made the four-hour journey eastward towards the Lowveld in the beautiful Mpumalanga Province of South Africa.

There we spent a few relaxing days at the guesthouse, sharing time with good friends. While we were there, Paul sought counsel from an older missionary friend. He was reticent to give Paul any advice and said, "I don't want to mess with the chemistry of your soul." In other words, he wanted to let the Holy Spirit direct Paul without his advice hindering the process. This counsel proved to be wise as God worked out His plan in our lives.

After a couple of days nothing significant had happened, and so we headed back home to Johannesburg. Our children were in their chairs on the backseat of the car sleeping. We had been driving for only half an hour or so when Paul looked at me and with enthusiasm blurted out, "I know what it is. I know what we are going to do."

I looked quizzically at him and implored, "Well, tell me!" With enthusiastic passion he pronounced, "We are going to start a missionary training college and it will be called Africa School of Missions (ASM). God is going to send out people from there to spread the gospel to the world."

The journey back seemed to fly by and when we arrived home, Paul rushed into his study and wrote out what God had dictated to his heart in the car on our journey back to Johannesburg. In the next few years, every single word written on those pieces of paper came to pass. They described the vision and the mission of the school in detail.

Paul was excited. He hardly slept. Every waking moment our conversation was infused with the vision that God had given us. Paul didn't understand everything that was happening in his heart, but he did feel a compulsion to go back to the Lowveld and look for a piece of property so that we could start this school.

One piece of information, crucial to this story, is that Paul and I had no resources with which to pursue this vision. We were still both young in years, but were so full of faith and confidence in the vision that God had given us that we made the four-hour journey back to that beautiful area. We also made an appointment with a real estate agent, asking him to show us some farms.

We booked into Come Together guesthouse again, and then full of anticipation and excitement, went to meet our real estate agent. He had selected a number of different properties for us to visit and we were keen to see each one.

We got to the first farm and the agent told Paul about the potential of the land and its productivity, as well as how many hectares the farm sat on and how much annual rainfall the farm received. As he rambled on, I walked up and down and claimed the land for Jesus.

We moved on to the next place, and the next.

It seemed that each one we went to was better than the previous one. And so I walked up and down, claiming the land for Jesus. By the end of the day Jesus, Paul, and I owned half of the land in the Lowveld!

Let me add an addendum here: Paul and I have never subscribed to the, "Health, Wealth, and Prosperity" doctrine. We cannot give credence to a teaching that God wants to give you every one of your earthly desires. God meeting our needs is different than Him granting us our desires and wants. In our view, that doctrine is unbiblical and selfish. However, we were young and inexperienced and we were also full of genuine, authentic faith.

Eventually, we did find a property that we thought was suitable for starting a missionary school and, after consulting with others about it, we decided to put in an offer on the land and the farmhouse. We then approached a builder and asked him how much it would cost to build forty dorm rooms on that property.

In retrospect this all appears almost reckless, as we did not have a penny to our name. But to us it was simple faith that God had spoken and that He would provide. All we had was a vision from God and a strong faith that if God is the Author of your vision, He will be the Provider of that vision.

A few days later, we received word from our agent that our offer on the property had been rejected. We both felt deflated because we believed

God had given us faith for that piece of land. We spent that evening at the guesthouse feeling quite dejected.

I was in the bathroom brushing my teeth when a Scripture verse came to my mind. Isaiah 55: 9 says, "As the heavens are higher than the earth, / so are my ways higher than your ways / and my thoughts than your thoughts." I knew that God had a significantly better plan than we did.

A peace flooded my heart from that moment. I shared the verse from Isaiah with Paul and told him that I felt that God had something much bigger and better than we could imagine. Since that day, I have always been aware that if God gives the vision, then He will make provision. And so we made the journey back to Johannesburg.

Paul was still feeling slightly despondent and so he gave his vision back to God. He said, "God, this is your vision and your plan, and I am now going to stop trying to make things happen. I give this vision back to you. If it takes three months or three years, I am going to rest in You and Your ability to see this vision fulfilled."

A few nights later, Paul received a phone call from a man he was not acquainted with. The man introduced himself by saying, "I hear you have a vision. I would like to come and talk to you about it." Paul invited the man to dinner a few nights later. I cooked a lovely roast chicken with all the trimmings.

Unfortunately, our guest arrived two hours later than the appointed time and so the chicken was shriveled, the vegetables were dried out, and the dessert was ruined. I was not very happy. However, our new friend ate the unappetizing fare with relish. All I could think was that he must be starving to eat up all that dried and insipid food.

After dinner, he took his coffee and sat with us while Paul shared his vision for training missionaries and sending them out across the world. By then we had learned that the man we were speaking to was a very successful and godly businessman. He listened intently to every word Paul spoke. He was a man of few words, so he did not say much; he simply asked us if he could bring his wife to meet us.

They came a week later, and once again we shared with her the passion and vision of our hearts. She listened as intently as her husband and then asked some poignant questions pertaining to our vision and how we would set about accomplishing our goals.

Some days later, we received a phone call from this same businessman. He said to Paul, "I am not sure if you know the Lowveld at all." Paul wanted to say, "Not only do I know it, but Jesus and Carol and I own half the land there!" The businessman continued, "I own two hotels there and I would like for you and your family to come down and spend a few days with us."

We stayed in their beautiful hotel on the top of a mountain, and as we looked down into the valley we saw another magnificent hotel that rested on fifty acres of land. It was beautiful, with a swimming pool, tennis courts, and over thirty rooms with adjoining bathrooms spread all over the well-manicured grounds. He showed it to us from the mountaintop and then told us he wanted to take us to see the property the next day.

Early mornings in South Africa are stunning. If you awaken with the dawn, you will experience some of the most magnificent sunrises. Colors of orange, peach, and mauve infuse the skies. If you sit long enough you can watch the sun slowly filter through the eucalyptus, acacia, and other indigenous trees. Their leaves soak up the sun's radiance seemingly changing their color.

Fortunate are you if you are privileged to catch a glimpse of a fish eagle soaring above the trees and hear its haunting song. If you don't hear the fish eagle, your ears will certainly reverberate with the sound of frogs and cicadas waking up to the dawn. It is a joyous cacophony. All your senses are enlivened at that moment as the sights, sounds, and smells of Africa hold you in their spell and you bask in the early morning hues of an African sunrise.

Africa has this way of mesmerizing you and holding you captive in its grip. It gets into your blood and no matter where you go on earth it will always beat inside your breast. A land of huge contrasts and disparities, but its beauty is in the soil and its people and there is no way Africa will ever let go of you.

On this particular morning, we made our way down to the Good News Centre on Peebles Road. It sat on fifty acres of lush green grass, hedged in by beautiful indigenous trees and shrubs and surrounded by the magnificent Petra Mountain. We had tea on the veranda and took in all the sweeping views of mountains and acres of eucalyptus trees that grew on the other side of the valley. It was a delightful spot on God's planet. We sat talking to our businessman friend about our vision and desire to train the next generation to serve Jesus around the world. He listened with intensity and our passion seemed to touch his heart.

I still recall the moment he looked at Paul and me and said, "God has given us confidence in your vision. We *do* believe that you will impact nations. And so, everything you see here, from the teaspoons in the kitchen to the tennis courts and the grounds—everything is yours to do what God has called you to do." That was one of the most amazing moments of our lives and we will never forget that day.

God's ways and thoughts are higher and significantly grander than ours could ever be. We have such limited perspectives of time and eternity, but God sees from beginning to end. Sometimes it seems as if God is getting it wrong, but He knows best because of His eternal perspective. We can trust Him.

At the beginning of January 1985 Africa School of Missions opened its doors to thirty-six intrepid students from all over South Africa and other countries of the world. The history of the school would have to be covered in another volume, but suffice it to say that over the next number of years we sent missionaries to over forty-seven nations around the world. That may not seem too phenomenal, but keep in mind that this was in the midst of the apartheid era when countries were still closing their doors to South Africans. It was also in a time when South Africa was *receiving* missionaries into our homeland, not sending them. So what we were doing seemed very audacious, and to some people even foolish.

I remember when we left Fairview one of our deacons said loudly enough for Paul and me to hear, "They are moving to White River to build a white elephant that will die in a year." I am happy to say that he was wrong and that Africa School of Missions is still training missionaries to this day. I am not certain what the last count was, but I do know that missionaries who have trained at ASM now serve God in well over sixty different countries of the world.

There were other wonderful provisions along the way—too many of them to be recounted in this book, but perhaps there is one that I should tell. The school was growing rapidly and with growth came both blessing and challenge. So as the student numbers rose, we needed more faculty and staff, and with people came the need for more buildings.

Paul went to his leadership team and recommended that the school consider taking out a loan with the bank. None of them were too enthusiastic about the proposal because we had never had to borrow money, and this would be a first. The number he proposed was staggering and almost too much for his team to comprehend.

I was at home at the time. Sitting on the edge of my bed I was reading from Isaiah 45 when I came across verses 2 and 3, which say:

> I will go before you
> and will level the mountains;
> I will break down gates of bronze
> and cut through bars of iron.
> I will give you hidden treasures,
> riches stored in secret places,
> so that you may know that I am the Lord,
> the God of Israel, who summons you by name.

As I read this passage, I felt it was a clear word to my heart that God was going to give us "treasures . . . stored in secret places." I was so convinced that I had heard God that I ran all the way from my house up to Paul's office, which was at least a quarter of a mile across the campus.

Barging right in, out of breath, I said, "Love, we don't have to take out a loan from the bank. God is going to give you money in Europe." (Paul was leaving the next day for a scheduled ministry trip to France and Germany).

I read him the verse from Isaiah and he looked at me quizzically and asked me, "Is this souls God is going to give us?"

I quickly responded, "No, it is money."

Although this might appear strange, let me assure you that I would have been content with God giving me this word for souls, but I knew He was telling me that He was going to provide for the buildings we needed to erect as a result of the growth at the college.

Paul went into our faculty and staff meeting on that day and told them what God had said to me. He put the verse up on our whiteboard and asked everyone to pray for him as he left for his trip. It was a bold step to take because, in essence, we were telling everyone that God was going to provide enough money to set up the buildings.

After a long and tiring flight, Paul arrived in Germany and was met by some staff members who were working at ASM but visiting Europe at that time. They informed him that a mutual friend wanted to have lunch with him. Paul, feeling tired after the journey, washed his face and straightened his hair, attempting to make himself presentable for the meeting.

Lunch was delightful. Our friend showed a keen interest in ASM, and Paul enthusiastically reported on growth and development. After the meal Paul was invited to the offices of this kind gentleman. He looked at Paul and said, "God has told me to sew a seed into your ministry." He informed Paul that he was not doing this because he had an abundance of finance, but because he was being obedient to God. He signed a check and handed it to Paul. Paul tried to be discreet and took the check and placed it in his pocket, to which our friend retorted, "No, no, you need to look at it!"

When Paul looked again it was for the exact amount of money he had told our leadership to borrow from the bank.

With the verse still on the whiteboard, and ringing in the ears of our staff and faculty, I was able to inform them at our meeting the next day that God had indeed answered that prayer. Wild hope saw us through ten incredible years at ASM with a lifetime of memories and the world impacted by God's amazing love and transforming message.

Reflection

Hudson Taylor was right when he said, "God's work done in God's way will never lack God's supply." Through all our years at ASM, we saw God provide in the most amazing ways. Sometimes He answered our prayer at midnight, but He always answered.

Hebrews 11:1 says, "Now faith is confidence in what we hope for and assurance about what we do not see." I do love the use of the word 'assurance' because it is pivotal to faith. We hope with certain assurance, which is what I call *wild hope*. If our hearts are filled with a wild hope for God's world, for our families and friends, there is no knowing what God can do. Let wild hope fill your heart for whatever challenge or dream is before you.

If you are in the midst of a trying time, let the hope of this text in Hebrews fill your heart and infuse your veins. Hope is not some kind of wishful thinking. In the biblical sense, hope is something much more than that. It is being certain that what we pray and long for will come to fruition.

The next chapter in the book of Hebrews exhorts us to keep our eyes fixed on Jesus. I am not sure where you are in your pilgrimage at this juncture. But I do know that if you keep your eyes on Jesus, the journey is made so much easier. I encourage you to keep focused on the goal; don't be distracted along the way, and He will see you through each stage of your pilgrimage.

There have been many aspects of my Christian walk that have been challenging. I would never choose to relive some of those seasons, but through every chapter of my journey God's hand has been involved in the smallest details.

I have often marveled at how God is intricately involved in all the aspects of my life. I knew I could trust God with this and the next season of my life. New challenges were around the corner, but they would further equip me to serve and love God's world.

 *Chapter 9*

God's Care in Troubled Kangwane

We must accept finite disappointment,
but never lose infinite hope.

MARTIN LUTHER KING JR.

HER VOICE WAS FRANTIC, PLEADING as she called out, "Mommy, Mommy, come quickly!" Panic-stricken, I rushed to my little girl's bedroom and found her huddled under her covers. My heart was racing as I pleaded with her to come out from under her blanket and tell me what was wrong. "I am scared of the witch doctor's drums. Mommy, please make them stop," she stammered with terror in her little voice.

If you have ever heard the beat of a witch doctor's drums, you will know how haunting and eerie that sound can be as it fills the air with a ghostly resonance. We once asked a witch doctor why he beat his drums for so long, and with glazed eyes and raspy voice he replied, "I beat the drums until they talk to me!" That sound can be hypnotic, but it is also eerie and sinister.

Night after night our children went to bed with the echoes of the witch doctor's drums rolling down the hill, penetrating the darkness, and making an unwelcome entrance into their bedrooms with a dissonant boom. It was an ominous sound that they would hear over and over while we lived at ASM.

The morning after this latest incident, I woke up determined that I would go and search for where the sound of those drums was coming from. I am not sure what possessed me other than a desire to appease my daughter's fears.

The college owned an old four-wheel-drive vehicle that had been given for ministry into the surrounding communities. After seeing my children safely off to school that morning, I got into the car and went in search of the witch doctor's drums.

It was still early in the morning, and the intense heat of the midday sun was not yet upon us. I drove out of our driveway and turned left onto the sand road that led out of ASM. I then made another left turn up the windy hill towards Kangwane. I was driving slowly and deliberately, trying to discern where the sound of those haunting drums had come from night after night. Eventually I made a right turn into the heart of Kangwane.

The road into the village was not paved and there were huge potholes along the way. Suddenly the atmosphere changed. There was no longer any beautiful flora lining the way as I drove along. The trees seemed to be wilting from lack of nourishment and water. And what was worse was that the atmosphere of hope and orderliness seemed to vanish in a cloud of dust and despair.

Fortunately, the vehicle I was driving was made for those unattended roads. I bumped up and down as fine dust filled the air and dried my mouth and nose. I sneezed and coughed simultaneously as the vehicle hiccupped over huge mounds and through cavernous potholes. I was grateful for the four-wheel drive that bore me safely along the littered roads—broken bottles, paper, feces from animals and humans were scattered over the street. The toxic smell of urine, discarded food, and waste filled the air with a nauseating stench.

As I drove farther along, taking in all the sights and sounds, I was horrified to see children of five and six years carrying little babies on their backs. It is a common sight to see an African mother carry her baby in this way. It simultaneously frees the mother's hands to enable her to accomplish her chores while the baby enjoys the close proximity to the mother as well as the rocking motion, which usually lulls the little one to sleep. But these were children, little ones themselves, barely off their own mother's backs. And yet they were caring for and carrying their tiny siblings.

I was aghast. I sat and watched as children walked the streets looking forlorn, hungry, and desperate. There was sadness in their eyes that made me cry. I drove a bit farther down the road and the scene intensified. Little ones in shabby clothing, no shoes to cover their little feet—their bellies distended from malnourishment and the onset of kwashiorkor—walked aimlessly down the dusty streets. My heart grieved.

I did not find the witch doctor or hear his drums that day. What I heard along that dusty, littered street that morning was the drumbeat of heaven. I followed those sounds into the heart of God where poverty, despair, and hunger had become part of the rhythm of life for so many children and families living in this tiny corner of God's universe.

I felt an ache in my heart so intense I knew it could only be the ache of the heart of God. And my only response was, "I must do something!" I didn't know what I could do or how I could do it, but I knew that I had to try.

Paul always rushed home from college at lunchtime. It was our hour together as a family and we all enjoyed chatting about the morning's happenings over a meal. Our children attended a little Christian school on campus and one of the benefits was lunching together in our home on a daily basis.

I loved to bake, and the aroma of fresh bread seemed to lure my family home no matter what exciting event was occurring on our campus at that hour. They were anxious to appease the pangs of hunger that had intensified during a busy morning and fill their bellies with homemade manna. With their hunger satisfied, they were ready to face the remainder of their day.

On this particular day, Paul looked for me in the kitchen where I was usually stationed over a steaming hot loaf of bread, carefully covering each slice with a generous portion of homemade butter. Paul did not find me in the kitchen that day; he found me in my living room distraught at what I had encountered on those dusty roads.

Neither of us had any idea what an incredible vision would grow from that tiny seed in my heart and the feeble cry of, "We must do something!" God loves to take the weak and minister into the bleakest places to bring hope to the needy. I offered myself to God that day to use me in any way that He could.

I do not want to sound like I am anyone special because I am not. And neither do I wish to credit myself with accomplishments that have had little to do with me. I only seek to point out that when we cry out to God, no matter how feeble and weak that cry might be, He will answer. I believe that there is no place so dark or barren, there is no hole so deep and dismal, and no sin so vile and detestable, that God's arm cannot extend to and His love cannot reach.

I responded immediately to what I had seen and encountered on that forlorn and dusty road. It resulted in a strategic visit to an African pastor in the heart of the neighborhood where the children lived. He had a very simple concrete block church with a tin roof. The building was stark, the walls were not painted, and the floors were made of cow dung. There were some wobbly wooden benches where older people could sit during the church service, but many adults and children generally sat on the floor.

I asked him if he would give me access to his church so that I could start a ministry for the needy children of his area. He was a kind and gracious old man with a beautifully weathered face and salt-and-pepper hair. He was probably not as old as he looked, but he walked with a shuffle, which was undoubtedly the result of a difficult life fraught with poverty. He was more than happy to oblige my request.

I found a wonderful young African lady who was willing to help me with this ministry. She had a round, happy face and her voluptuous figure seemed to dance wherever she went. She loved children and had a desire to see their lives improved.

Together we went to see some of the neighboring farmers to ask them if they would part with their over-ripe bananas. Since they could not be sold at the market the farmers were willing to let us have boxes of their slowly decaying fruit. And that was how we managed to feed the two hundred children who came to the little concrete block church every Monday through Friday morning.

The air was polluted with germs and a sense of despair and hopelessness, and the only way I could sanitize it was to try and fill it with hope. I wanted to help them to believe in a brighter future and a better tomorrow.

An army of children would attend our Care Center each day. Many of them were stark naked and those fortunate enough to have clothes usually wore tattered, filthy rags. Their unwashed bodies carried with them a pungent odor that floated around them like a noxious cloud. Their little heads were infested with invisible armies of preying lice. The wingless little parasites would feast on the blood of the starving children and further their discomfort with perpetually itching scalps. They would scratch endlessly and this would often lead to infection. Their plight was dismal.

My deepest desire was to wrap these children in my arms and bathe them with love. The children were hungry for touch, but some would recoil from human contact, afraid that it might bring a lashing or some other kind of abuse. Others would revel in an embrace and hold on for as long as possible.

At this time, around 1986, HIV and AIDS were beginning to manifest in our area. Of course, the problem has escalated over the years and Sub-Saharan Africa has the most serious HIV and AIDs epidemic in the world. Statistics are often unreliable, but some sources say that as many as twenty-five million people in Sub-Saharan Africa live with HIV. That accounts for nearly 70 percent of the global total. Staggering indeed!

Some of the debaucheries that occurred in our nation at this time and later were beyond belief. One of the most horrendous things happening in that part of the world was when some witch doctors informed people suffering with HIV or AIDS that the cure was to have sex with a virgin under the age of six.

When I visited South Africa in later years, I could not watch the news or read the newspaper because they told stories of men raping defenseless children and tiny babies. I know that this is distressing and disturbing information. I take no satisfaction in sharing these details. My hope is that as you read this, you will pause to pray for these vulnerable children and say, "We must do something," as I did so many years ago. You may not be able to go, but you can still do something.

Our meetings at the Care Center were simple. We would sing a few SiSwati songs and then with the help of my African friend translating for me, I would tell the children a Bible story. When story time was over, the children would go outside and wash their hands and faces in a tub of cold water. Water was precious, and we had to conserve every drop, so all two hundred children washed their hands in the same big tub. Once that task was finished, they ate over-ripe bananas (some children were so hungry they even ate the banana skin!) drank a cup of cold water, and then played outside for a short while.

The children never played for long. I soon realized it was not because they didn't enjoy playing, it was simply that they were so malnourished they just did not have energy for play. I remember looking into their eyes and seeing emptiness such as I had never seen before. My thought then (and now) was that no child should ever have to live in poverty and sadness. Every child should have the opportunity to live in safety and security and be loved. I felt helpless, and truth be told, I often felt hopeless.

We went into Kangwane week after week. There were just two of us involved in this ministry and it was tiring and at times discouraging. Political tension was rapidly mounting in our area. During the 1980s our nation was going through tremendous political turmoil and this area was no exception.

We were hearing stories of cars being over turned, people being killed, their homes pillaged and rummaged. The country was reeling from political unrest in the cities, where people were dying daily in riots. The pervasive unrest was filtering back into the homelands and the area where I was ministering. There are some incidents that are too horrendous for me to mention, but there was much suffering all over our nation.

One day, as I was driving back from the church on my own, a group of thugs tried to stop my vehicle on the road. I had the presence of mind to keep the engine running and continue driving slowly and deliberately even though they were standing across the road trying to block my access.

I kept advancing slowly forward, praying as I went. I did understand some of the words they were speaking in their native tongue. "*Bulala, bulala!*" the young men were chanting, "Kill, kill the white woman!" I eventually managed to get past the group and got out of Kangwane as quickly as possible. I reached home shaking and trembling; the full realization of what had occurred and the threat of death hitting me hard.

The following day the pastor from the church in Kangwane came to visit Paul and me. He told me not to go back to the area until it settled down; he felt the political tension was mounting and that more devastation would follow.

I had been ready to go into Kangwane that particular day. However, after the pastor suggested that I not return for a few weeks, I accepted his judgments, realizing that he had a far better understanding of the people and culture of his village than I did.

He then said to me; "Last night some thugs [probably the same people who had held up my vehicle] told me they were going to come to my church, lock you and all the children inside the building, and set you all on fire."

I really thought it was an idle threat, and simply said, "All right, I will give it a few weeks and let things settle down before returning."

That night some young men went to his house and murdered him and I never saw that pastor again. I am certain that if he had not warned me of impending doom, I would have gone in to Kangwane and the young men would have carried out their threat.

I never did go back and minister in that village again. Some months later, World Vision approached me with regard to taking over the ministry. With all their resources and their rich experience I felt it was a step in the right direction for the ministry and the well-being of the children. I moved into other aspects of ministry, but never lost my love for the children and a deep and intense desire for the well-being of girls and boys everywhere.

I planted a small seed that has grown into something beyond our wildest dreams. I certainly do not want to take credit for what has been accomplished. My part in the grander plan of God seems insignificant in the light of the needs of Africa. However, that little work spawned a desire in some students' hearts to make a difference in that area.

Many of our ASM graduates started ministries that have had a profound impact not only in Mpumalanga, but also all over Africa. We started a school of health at ASM and have seen it grow into an incredible ministry that has equipped hundreds of nurses who care for the sick and needy.

Other graduates began work among orphans that has had huge impact for the gospel. A clinic was pioneered at our college that has treated thousands of sick men, women, and children. Only eternity will tell how many lives have been impacted and saved.

Sometimes we look for the beating drums in the wrong places. Often those drums are beating in the slums, in the quagmire of sin and poverty—places we would not willingly go. Places and people who are desperate for wild hope!

Reflection

At times the needs of our world can appear overwhelming and a sense of desperation can invade our hearts bringing with it hopelessness. As Martin Luther King Jr said, if we lose hope we lose everything.

I cannot remember where I read this little story, but it is worth repeating. At the end of World War II, when the Allied forces in Germany were looking for snipers, they came across an old farmhouse. They went inside and saw that someone had written some words on the wall. They went as follows: "I believe in the sun even when it does not shine. I believe in love even when it is not shown. I believe in God even when He does not speak." Beauty and wild hope emanated from someone's soul even in the midst of bleakness and death. I believe that is the sort of hope that should infuse Christians.

Yes, we live in a world that is needy and at times desperate. I do believe, however, that every one of us can play a part in making it a better place. Each one of us can do something. What we cannot afford to do is to remain uninvolved. We must also resist making excuses. It is easy to say, "That is Africa or Asia, and I live too far away." That may be the case, but you can pray, or you can give in different ways.

I have always believed that all children everywhere should have warmth, security, shelter, and an abundance of love. We know that there are many children all over the world who have none of these.

Mother Teresa was once asked how she fed all the hungry children of the world. She replied that she fed them one at a time. Start with caring for one child. Perhaps there is a child on your street or in your neighborhood or a surrounding area to whom you can show God's love. Pray about the needs and ask God how you can join Him in bringing wild hope to this world.

The Bible says in 1 Corinthians 15:58 that, "Your labor in the Lord is not in vain." This means everything we do here on earth will count in eternity. Our work is not simply a waste of time and although we do not know how the lyrics we create or the children we care for or the books we write or the hungry we feed or the meals we cook or the unjust cause we speak up for will play out in eternity, we do know that God sees everything.

As we moved on from this chapter in our lives, God was opening other avenues to us. There were some deep, dark tunnels ahead that we knew nothing about, but God had an amazing way of preparing our hearts for all that was in store. I would need grace for what lay ahead and the wild hope that had infused me in my ministry life.

 *Chapter 10*

Bad News at the Front Door

Trials teach us what we are; they dig up the
soil, and let us see what we are made of.

CHARLES SPURGEON

AFTER NINE AMAZING YEARS AT ASM, we left our homeland for Brisbane, Australia. We had always made it our practice to include our children in the major decisions of our lives. Generally, we would hold a family meeting. There was a certain amount of ceremony involved in these occasions. Paul would buy some delicious pastries, I would brew a nice pot of tea, and we would sit down in our living room. Whenever this happened, the children always knew that something important was going to be discussed.

An opportunity had presented itself to lead a great Australian church and help establish a Bible college in South East Queensland. This meant leaving our homeland and our beloved ASM. It was no small decision and we all felt the emotion associated with such a significant intercontinental move. However, after much prayer and consultation, the four of us agreed that God was opening this new door and we all felt peace about going through with it.

Still, when we boarded the flight for Brisbane, Australia, I left a piece of my heart in Africa. Once the dust of Africa is in your blood, it will linger there for all time. It is amazing how the sights, sounds, and smells of that land hold you captive in its grip. I knew that memories were all I could take with me from this continent of such extremes.

Memory is an incredible gift. One moment a scent can trigger a feeling of contentment and delight, and the next second a story can surface that makes you weep. I am grateful for every memory—the good and the sad. Memories of Africa will always fill my heart with every type of human emotion.

Africa can be a harsh continent; war, famine, political instability, and AIDS have ravaged it. It is not a place for the fainthearted. But if it is in your blood, it will hold on to you with tenacity. Although this was not the first time Paul and I had left our homeland, we knew we would never return to live there again. My heart ached.

We arrived in Brisbane, Australia, early in the morning in the first week of January 1994. I remember stepping off the plane. The heat was so forceful it felt like a blast from a furnace hitting me with unrelenting force. It was only six-twenty a.m. I could not begin to comprehend what it would feel like at noon!

We were welcomed by a number of the staff and congregation of Glad Tidings City Church, and thus began over six years of happy ministry in Australia. The welcome was unique, and although we spoke a common language, it would take some time getting acquainted with the many Australian colloquialisms. "Welcome to Aussie!" one of the pastors said as he wrapped Paul in a backslapping embrace. "How ya going, mate?" said another, "Pretty hot, huh?" To which we all added our voices of agreement. "No worries. She'll be apples, mate!" he continued. I quickly realized we weren't being offered apples, we were simply being informed that everything would be all right. I do think Aussies have more colloquialisms than any other people and you probably need an Australian dictionary in the first year of life down under.

We enjoyed our time in Australia and made some lifelong friends. However, Australia felt like a detour. God used it to teach us some leadership lessons that we would probably not have learned in any other setting. But we never felt a sense of destiny; we knew our time there would be for a limited period.

The church we led was an established church that had been around for many years. In fact, William Booth Clibborn, great grandson of William Booth, who was the founder of the Salvation Army, pioneered it in 1930. He started a revival campaign in a tent and in the first year over eight hundred people made a decision for the Lord.

If you speak to people today, they will say that they have never experienced anything quite like they did in the days of William Booth Clibborn.

When we got to Glad Tidings, it was sixty years old. With age come challenges. And we had our fair share of them during our time there. Today we look back with gratitude at the Australian detour and believe that the lessons learned held us in good stead for what lay before us.

After living in Brisbane for three years, we built a beautiful home. One of the reasons we had built our home was so that my ageing parents could leave South Africa and come and live with us. My sister Gaille and her husband and family had recently moved to Brisbane, and we were able to get visas for our parents to join us. So we built a lovely and spacious "granny flat" above our house for my parents.

I enjoyed my home and the beautiful surroundings. Our house was perched on a lovely piece of land with a rippling stream that ran through the bottom of our yard. There was a cluster of Australian eucalyptus trees on our property that was home to chattering parakeets, laughing kookaburra, and a host of perpetually chirping rainbow lorikeets. Bird life in Australia is spectacular!

Paul had felt a burden for Europe for over twenty years, and while we were in Australia, this intensified. One morning, while Paul was away for a couple of weeks visiting Europe, I was sitting on my patio with a cup of tea and a book. We had only been living in our new home for three months. I was reading Billy Graham's autobiography *Just As I Am*.

Warm sunlight filtered through the eucalyptus trees and their leaves danced in the gentle breeze. I was soaking in the warm glow of an early morning, breathing in the distinct earthy fragrance of the Australian bush, and reveling in the chirping and singing of the birds. As I read, I sensed the Lord speak to my heart. *"Do you love Me more than this?"* He asked. I looked around at my house and answered with passion, "Lord, I love you much more than this home!" I felt God say, *"You will be leaving it very soon."*

At that time in our lives, Paul and I had not discussed leaving the church. We had just built our house, and our purpose was to stay for a few more years. However, I knew that God had spoken to my heart and that this house would not be my home for very long. Of course, I felt a tinge of sadness and remorse. We had so many wonderful friends, my parents were living with us, we had a comfortable home, and Australia is a magnificent country. This was not going to be easy.

One of the first things we do when Paul arrives home from a trip is to make a cup of tea and sit and chat about everything that has happened while we've been apart from each other.

We were sitting on our patio drinking our steaming hot cup of tea when Paul said in a serious tone, "I need to speak to you, love!" I looked at him and smiled. I had a sense that God had been dealing with both of our hearts simultaneously. I wanted to make this conversation easy for him, so I said, "Can I go first?"

With a sense of relief, he responded, "Yes! Go right ahead."

I told him how I had been sitting on our patio early one morning when God spoke to my heart. I explained how God had asked me the question, *"Do you love Me more than this home,"* and told Paul my response. I said to Paul with confidence that I knew God was leading us in a new direction.

He smiled reassuringly and replied, "I should never doubt that God always clarifies His voice in your heart as well as mine." We both knew that our time in Brisbane was coming to an end.

Once again, the move involved our family ceremony of pastries, tea, and much deliberating. Initially, we wondered if Anna and Jay wanted to stay on in Australia to complete their university studies and continue living in Brisbane. However, after much prayer they both decided to make the move with us, and we were delighted.

Anna had enjoyed Australia, but Jay never truly settled and his heart struggled to make it home. When we left Australia for the United States after six and a half years in Australia, there was no one happier than him.

On a cold Brisbane morning in July 2000, after serving at Glad Tidings City Church for almost seven years, we boarded a plane once more. Again the airport was packed with people. However, this time it was to say good-bye—the strangers that had greeted us on that hot, humid day when we arrived in Australia had now become wonderful friends and the farewells were not easy.

The greatest sadness in leaving Brisbane was saying good-bye to my parents. They are two of the most remarkable people I know. Both of them are flexible and adaptable and share a love for life that rivals the most jovial of people. My parents have an inner contentment that can only be defined as godly satisfaction.

As I've said before, good-byes are part of the rhythm of our lives and yet they never get any easier with the passing of time. The only joy coming from that farewell has been that we have been able to fly my parents out to the States on a number of occasions and spend lengthy time with them when they visit.

More than anyone else that morning, Jay was filled with excitement. He had visited the US with us on many occasions. However, one of Jay's most memorable and happy times was when he left school and traveled around the world with his best friend, Mark.

One of their final destinations was the US, and that particular visit had such a profound effect on Jay that he pronounced with unwavering boldness to Mark, "One day I am going to live in California." Jay remembered it well because he was sitting in a Starbucks and Mark jokingly responded, "And one day I am going to live on the moon!" Mark never thought that Jay would leave Australia.

We arrived in the States to a church which had kindly offered us the use of a house and some office space. The idea was that we would travel in and out of Europe, but we would have a home base and a church to attend when we were not traveling.

We were based in the Windy City of Chicago. Jay went to university in Minneapolis, Minnesota, and Anna went to university in Springfield, Illinois.

When Jay phoned me for the first time from his university, he said, "Mom, I have come home! My heart is at home." Nothing warms a mother's heart more than a happy child!

We loved Chicago. There was so much to do and see. We would stroll on Michigan Avenue, visit the many cultural institutions and museums, walk around Navy Pier, and enjoy the buzz of a vibrant city. We were in and out of Europe countless times during the year, teaching and promoting missions.

It was a wonderful season in our lives, and we enjoyed every moment of our time. Anna and Jay were both happy at their universities and both of them were making great friends. As a family, we were all prospering in our souls. For a Christian wife and mother, the happiness of her family is one of her main priorities.

After being in Chicago for almost two years, we were invited to visit a church in Concord, North Carolina. Our friend Sam Farina was the pastor at that time, and we were asked to share a weekend of ministry in his church.

North Carolina is a beautiful state, rich in cultural and natural beauty.

I recall the first time we drove the Blue Ridge Parkway; our breath was taken away by the stunning vistas of rugged mountains and the beautiful Appalachian countryside. The road winds for 469 miles through the mountains. One moment you drive through cottonlike mist, and then the road twists and winds around a bend and you suddenly break through the fog into a cathedral of green oaks and sycamore trees. Rhododendron—particularly spectacular in spring—lines the parkway.

On February 1, 2002, we moved into a new home in Concord, North Carolina. We had accepted the invitation to go and help with the mission program at Concord First Assembly church. The leaders were generous and enabled us to maintain a heavy travel schedule in Europe.

We loved being at First Assembly, and the people were welcoming and hospitable. Jay had decided that he wanted to leave his university in Minneapolis and pursue a degree in cultural anthropology at a school in California. We were never quite sure whether it was the degree he was pursuing or the weather and the surf on the West Coast. However, he was persuasive enough for us to agree that he could transfer, and so he finished his time in Minneapolis in December and traveled with us to North Carolina. Anna was pursuing a dual degree in general education and special education and loved every minute of her studies. She was quite content to stay where she was.

I recall leaving Chicago carpeted in snow and arriving to a beautiful, balmy seventy degrees in Concord. I thought I was in heaven. Now my sun-deprived frame could thaw out and soak in the sun. I loved snow, but enough was enough.

Jay was due to start his studies in California, in August, and so he got a job to save for the expensive trip and to cover some of his tuition costs. He had not enjoyed the cold weather in Minneapolis and declared that he would never live in the north again. He was anxious to get to California.

We loved the mild winter in North Carolina, but the spring was spectacular as the sun bathed our yard, inducing all the fragrances of spring. White blossoms splashed all over the dogwood trees, forming a cloudlike canopy. A plethora of petals draped the rhododendron and fell to the ground in a carpet of pink, while the sweet fragrance of honeysuckle seeped through the windows, filling our home with their scent. Large oak and maple trees, forming a thick veil of green, sheltered us from suburbia. We felt as if we were living in our own private forest.

One day in spring I received a phone call from Anna. She was happy and chirpily proclaimed, "Mom, God has really been speaking to me."

She had my attention!

She went further. "I have this sense that something is going to happen this summer and I feel I should prepare my heart for whatever it is." She had been reading consistently through her Bible and spending more time with the Lord. I encouraged her that day in that pursuit and then didn't give much thought to it again. However, Anna was earnest in her devotion, and wherever she went in her car, she listened to praise and worship music and tried to prepare her heart for what God had in store.

Summer arrived with a vengeance, and the year 2002 was a particularly scorching one in North Carolina. Anna came home for the summer break, and it was wonderful to all be together again. She worked through the summer with a friend of ours so that she could pay off some of her tuition and have some spending money. We were all busy, but we were enjoying evenings and weekends together.

On Monday morning, June 24, 2002, Anna came downstairs looking washed out and pale. "Mom," she cried, "I don't feel well." I began with my long list of maternal questions regarding her state of health. After answering each one, I determined that there was nothing significantly wrong with her and that she should eat breakfast and see how she felt afterward.

Anna tried eating some breakfast, but found it unpalatable, so she drank her tea and left for work. Every day of that week she felt she couldn't face food. She said she had no pain or nausea, but she simply didn't feel like eating. I said jokingly, "Maybe God has you on a forced fast." We chuckled, but the situation remained the same for that entire week.

Wednesday morning, June 26, just before Anna was due to leave for work, she looked out of her bedroom window and saw her brother driving off in his black convertible Ford Mustang. Suddenly her stomach tightened like a clenched fist and waves of nausea swept through her body. She wanted to open her window and scream, "Jay, come back, you are going to have an accident!" However, he came home an hour later. She chided herself severely and quietly told herself, "Get a grip!"

Friday evening, June 28, Anna had a strange and unusual experience. Let me state from the outset that I have no way of explaining this experience theologically. All I know is that my daughter is a profoundly practical girl with a level head and two feet firmly planted on terra firma. And I do believe that God is sovereign and He knows all things.

Anna was sitting watching television while I prepared dinner in the kitchen. Her brother was out at work. She was watching the news when suddenly and with absolute clarity she recalls seeing a headline announcing: "A black Ford Mustang has been hit by a truck and the driver is fighting for his life." The accident appeared before her eyes and she saw a truck had rolled over on top of the car. Her heart hammered in sheer terror as fear grabbed her by the throat. She turned around hastily to cry, "Mom, I think Jay has been in an accident," when Jay breezed through the back door and greeted us cheerfully.

We know now that there was no accident that Friday evening and Anna had obviously seen a vision. She was so shaken that she took herself upstairs on wobbly legs to calm down. She did not say anything to either Jay or me for fear of us thinking she was silly. When Paul arrived home, the three of us ate dinner together (Anna still could not face food) and the remainder of our evening was uneventful.

On Sunday evening, June 30, we were all in church as a family. A friend of mine distinctly recalls looking at me and beginning to weep. As she wept, she prayed that the Lord would help and give me grace for the coming season. She simply did not understand why she was so emotional.

Anna got home that night and wrote in her journal, "God, I do not know what is going on with me. I do not understand these strange experiences. But I ask you to put your arms of protection around my brother." And then she fell asleep.

On Monday morning, July 1, 2002, Anna bounced downstairs and with a lilt in her voice said, "Mom, I feel great and I'm really hungry!" For the first time in seven days Anna ate food. Jay joined us for the meal and cheerfully declared, "Mom, you make the best cheese-and-tomato sandwiches in the world!"

Anna left for work and soon after she had gone Jay got up from the table to leave. As he was going out the back door, he looked back at me and said, "Love you more than life itself!" And he was gone.

I remember it was a scorching day. As I left the house and went outside, heat washed over me and sweat poured down my body within seconds. Sticky droplets ran down my neck and made my hair cling to my skin. I remember that year because our beautiful green lawn had turned yellow from the scorching rays of the sun and the continual lack of rain. It felt good to get into the car and feel cold air blow over me and cool me down.

Many chores needed to be accomplished on that particular day, and one of them was to restock the pantry and the fridge. So off to the supermarket I went. I strode purposefully down the aisles thinking about my weekly menu and filling my basket with my family's favorite foods.

I love to cook and my family loves to eat. They have always shown appreciation for the effort I put into making their meals. No one was more appreciative than Jay, whose appetite was ferocious! He was running a five-minute mile, playing soccer, and working out at the gym. All of this activity called for copious amounts of food to fill the constant hunger in his belly. It seemed an impossible task!

I got home from my shopping expedition and unloaded the groceries, carefully packing them away in the pantry and fridge. I took salmon out the freezer for dinner and then put the coffeepot on. I generally have one cup of coffee a day. The acrid liquid initially did nothing for my taste buds, but I discovered that by adding lavish amounts of cream to the bitterness, the flavor is greatly enhanced and delightful for the palate. More than one cup a day would be detrimental for my morning weigh-in, though, and the scale would quickly scream at me to curb my intake.

I was about to get my coffee and go and sit on my back porch to read my Bible when the doorbell disturbed my rhythm. I muttered something about the untimeliness of the person ringing the bell as I went to answer it. But I smiled as I opened the door to a big, burly police officer.

Thoughts were tumbling around my brain. *I wonder what he wants?* Then the ah-ha moment! *Ah, yes, he wants my money. Must be collecting for the police force.* The terrorist attack of September 11 was still fresh in everyone's minds and there was a constant flow of people asking for money for the police and fire departments.

As I stood there, he interrupted my thoughts by inquiring, "Are you Mrs. Alexander?"

I responded quizzically, "Yes!"

"Do you have a son, Jason Alexander?"

Now my mind was working quickly. I wondered if Jay had been caught going over the speed limit. I thought, *Wow! The laws in North Carolina are weird. Why must a police officer come to my door to inform me of a speeding offence?* That was the sum total of what I was anticipating on this hot summer day of July 1, 2002.

Before I could question the police officer, words began pouring out of his mouth. " I have some bad news for you, ma'am."

I thought, I *don't want your bad news, so buzz off and take it with you!*

But the words kept coming. Slowly and deliberately they fell from his lips, hitting me with the force of a ton of bricks. "I am so sorry. Your son has been involved in a tragic motor-vehicle accident. He has been airlifted to a hospital in Charlotte."

I stood there in stunned silence. Instantly the world stopped. The police officer's lips were moving, but I could not hear anything. I was surrounded by darkness and intense quiet. Then suddenly, with brutal force, the words seemed to batter my consciousness and bring me back to the awful moment of reality staring me between the eyes.

Tears I had no control over streamed down my face, running down my neck and wetting the collar around my dress. My hands shook. My stomach churned, and fear like wildfire charged relentlessly through my body. "Is he okay? Tell me, is he okay?" I pleaded.

"Ma'am," the police officer replied regretfully. "He was not breathing when the emergency vehicle got to him. But they managed to get a breathing tube down his throat and he is being transported by helicopter to the hospital as we speak." Each word was emphasized with a staccatolike clip. When he said, "You need to get to the hospital quickly," I knew the situation was desperate.

I implored him, "Can you please wait with me while I phone my husband?" He was kind and gracious and stood indoors with me while I phoned Paul.

The phone in my hand shook with an intensity that astonished me. It rang a few times before Paul's familiar voice answered cheerfully. "Hello!"

For some reason I could not repeat the words the police officer had said to me. I simply could not say those words out loud.

With a trembling voice I hardly recognized as my own, I said, "Love, Jay has had an accident, and he has been taken to hospital."

Paul could hear I was shaken, and he replied with empathy, "Love, control yourself. It will be fine."

How could I tell Paul that our only son, our precious boy, was fighting the greatest battle of his life and he might not make it through the next hour? My hands trembling, I handed the phone to the police officer and asked him to tell Paul which hospital Jay was in. I had not heard the details clearly and I felt the back of my throat burning as I tried to swallow the salty tears that refused to stay down.

The police officer gave Paul the address of the hospital and then passed the phone back to me. Paul spoke soothingly and reassuringly to me. "Sam and I will come as soon as possible."

Paul was out having lunch with our pastor and friend, Sam Farina. Obviously the reality of the situation had not yet registered, because it seemed like forever before they showed up. I phoned Paul ten minutes later and with sheer desperation pleaded, "Where are you?"

Paul replied, "We're on our way. Sam was held up with some parishioners." Clearly the urgency of our situation had not sunk in.

I was a bit more cognizant at that moment, and with agony in my voice I said, "Love, it is bad. It's very bad. Jay had to be taken to the hospital by helicopter."

I heard a gasp and then, "Jesus, Jesus, Jesus!" was all that Paul managed to utter. They arrived a few minutes later to make the agonizing drive to the hospital in Charlotte and see what awaited us.

Fear settled on me like a dark cloud, and with it came an agony that is difficult to articulate. I perceived that the worst pain was the one I could not glimpse—the one on the horizon, like a thunderstorm brewing in the sky. I could sense the tempest was at hand, and with it pain would come like a flood. I felt helpless.

As Sam drove us to the hospital, I phoned our precious Anna to tell her that her brother had been involved in a horrific car accident. She sobbed uncontrollably and the anguish in her voice made me want to protect her from the horror we were all confronting. I could not. We could not run from this, hide from it, or will it away. This was our reality and we had to face it.

Our long nightmare had just begun.

Jay's accident on July 1, 2002, changed our lives forever. The impact on Jay's car was so great it sheared the wheels from the axles.

Reflection

As I reflect on this time in my life, I must be honest and say I felt the intensity of my humanity. Fear seemed to seep from every pore in my body as we made that drive to the hospital. Because I am a Christ follower does not mean that I do not suffer pain. It also does not mean that bad things do not happen to me.

Life is full of mysteries. There are some questions that hang in the air like mist on a cloudy day. There are times when situations make no sense at all. Many people have puzzled over the question *Why do bad things happen to good people?* Job asked that question and so do many of the psalms. People ask that when there is a tragedy, an earthquake, a war, or famine.

I have pondered this question, and although I do not have all the answers, I do think that the Bible does give us help. Jesus always told the truth, and unlike some religious leaders who try to dismiss pain and suffering, Jesus said in John 16:33, "In this world you will have trouble." We live in an imperfect world and because of that we will experience pain and suffering. Let me share a few truths (and some of my thinking here is influenced by a sermon I heard, but I cannot remember who preached it), as I reflect back on this time in our lives.

First, God did not create a world of pain and suffering. The book of Genesis, which is the first book of the Bible, tells us that in the beginning God made everything good. God made a wonderful and perfect world that was later corrupted by sin.

Much of our suffering is the result of our choices and the things we do or do not do. Many of the wars that have been fought have been due to the actions of evil and immoral leaders. They have caused untold suffering to thousands because of their greed and lust for power and control.

God gave man free will, and unfortunately, some have used that free will in a corrupt and abusive way. Many people around the globe suffer hunger on a daily basis. How can we blame God for this? The world produces enough food to feed everyone and yet still many go hungry. Once again, it is an abuse of wealth and power. It seems to me, that the root of many of our problems is the love of power and money—they can be extremely corrupting forces.

Second, God can bring good out of suffering. Romans 8:28 says, "And we know that in all things God works for the good of those who love him, who have been called according to his purpose." God does not create suffering and pain, but He can bring good out of our pain. I have seen people go through incredible suffering and come through it in a remarkable way. They have been able to use their pain to help countless other people in their difficulty.

Third, one day all suffering will come to an end. That will be a wonderful day, and in the light of eternity all of our sufferings will pale in comparison. Suffering can make us better people. Our pain can have one of two effects: it can make us bitter people or it can make us better. It is our choice.

On the worst day of my life, God reminded me of the familiar scripture in Psalm 139:16 that encouraged me that God knew about this moment in my life. Although I was taken by surprise, He was not. He knows what tomorrow holds, and whatever it brings with it, He will sustain us through those times.

If you are going through a desperate and difficult time, I pray that you will take courage in Him. I know God walked with me through my darkest night, and He will journey with you. Amazingly, through some of the most desperate moments of that season, God filled me with hope so profound I knew it could only be from Him. I trust that a wild hope will fill your heart for whatever you are facing.

 Chapter 11

God's Enfolding Arms in Trauma Intensive-Care

Suffering becomes beautiful when anyone bears
great calamities with cheerfulness, not through
insensibility but through greatness of mind.

ARISTOTLE

WE UNBUCKLED OUR SEAT BELTS before we arrived at the front door of the hospital. Our legs carried us swiftly to the front door of the Emergency entrance. We stumbled up to the reception desk to see if someone could help us. The policeman had said, "When you get to the hospital, tell them you are the mother of the injured boy who was flown in by helicopter."

With a trembling voice I repeated those words to the lady at the front desk. Lips pursed with empathy, she uttered, "Is the policeman here to identify the body with you?" (I am still not sure why she asked this question.)

Hot salty tears flowed shamelessly down my cheeks as I collapsed into a chair. "Identify my son's body?" The thought shot through my mind, *Why would you need the policeman to identify "the body" unless he is dead?* I promptly pushed that thought away and shuddered, then got up and began to pace up and down the room.

If you can possibly believe it, we heard nothing for at least twenty minutes, and those were some of the most agonizing moments of my life. Paul was frantic—at one point he looked at someone and with a voice filled with desperation implored, "Tell me if my son is alive . . . please?"

Eventually two grim-faced doctors walked down the hallway and introduced themselves to Paul and me. They invited Pastor Sam to accompany us to a cold, dismal little room down the stark corridor. We collapsed onto a sofa, utterly distraught.

The doctors pulled no punches. "Your son is in critical condition. Every organ in his body is ruptured, and we need to take him upstairs for surgery."

My heart soared—surgery meant there was still hope!

They continued speaking, emphasizing their words, knowing they were offending our ears as they spoke and we listened. "We must be honest and tell you that people with your son's injuries do not survive." Their words were brutal; like a hammer they knocked our spirits down blow by forceful blow.

Paul went white and I could see the nerves twitch at the corners of his mouth as fear spread across his face. He excused himself from the room. Later he told me he stood over the toilet bowl and retched.

Then, gathering himself together, he splashed cold water on his face and walked back into the room. Pain was etched in his features, and it made me cry.

Our daughter arrived with our friend Dean, and they both sat down in that stark little room.

Agony penciled across her brow and tears welled in her eyes as she listened to the incredible list of injuries her brother had sustained. He had a ruptured liver, spleen, and lungs, and every rib in his body was broken. All the experiences Anna had gone through from the springtime until this very day suddenly made sense to her.

The doctors told us to go to the fifth floor and wait there until we got further news.

We ventured out of that depressing room and into the light. Anna was crying, and tears streamed down my face like a leaky tap that would not be stopped. My legs were shaky as we made our way down the corridor.

Anna paused to steady me, and then she put both her hands on my shoulders and said slowly and deliberately, "Mommy, my brother is not going to die. He is going to walk out of this hospital!"

I don't know why, but I believed her words more than I did those knowledgeable and professional doctors. It is not that I have ever undermined the medical profession. I am eternally grateful for them and believe that God used those gifted men and women through our terrible tragedy. But when Anna spoke to me, a quiet hope seemed to filter through my veins, and although the pain did not cease and fear did not diminish, I believed that one day Jay would walk out of that hospital.

Wild hope!

Slowly we walked up the stairs and then down the long grey corridors, passing nurses in their colorful scrubs and doctors in starched white coats. They all seemed a blur to me.

My world was spinning out of control, in absolute upheaval, while people strode calmly and deliberately down the halls, oblivious to the nightmare we were facing.

We made it to the fifth-floor waiting room and found it packed with people from our church. We had only been at First Assembly for five months and yet the room was filled from corner to corner with people to support us. I was overwhelmed.

Sometimes people say that God is silent, but in the darkest night God screams at you through your pain. And His love and grace were loudly manifested through His people that day. As I reflect back over that time, I know our gracious God showed us His love, and it echoed over and again from every corner of the world. The body of Christ may be flawed, but when my life is coming apart, there is no other community in the world I would rather be part of than the church.

We sat there waiting. I was acutely aware of every organ, muscle, and sinew in my body. My head throbbed, my throat was tight, my mouth dry. My stomach felt sick, my knees were weak, and my heart was aching. I was in a vortex.

A thoracic and cardiac surgeon came to speak to us. His voice threaded with urgency, he said, "We have discovered that your son has a ruptured aorta. We are not sure how he has survived to this point, but we need you to sign these release forms so that we can go in and perform surgery on him immediately."

I thought, *How many more injuries will they discover?* I was yet to find out.

The percentage rate of patients who survive traumatic ruptured aortic injuries is dismal. Jay had sustained numerous other injuries as well, so his chances of survival were less than slim. Paul signed the release forms, and then Sam went and asked the cardiologist if he could pray with him before they went into surgery.

The cardiac surgeon nodded. "I would be grateful."

Our hearts were never more earnest than when we said amen to that prayer. The long strides and hurried pace with which the cardiologist exited our room revealed the urgency and the seriousness of the task before him.

Jay's accident made it to all the news channels, and the next day his story was on the front page of the *Charlotte Observer* and the *Independent Tribune*. The details emerged. Jay had been sitting at a notoriously dangerous and accident-prone intersection on Weddington and Pitt School Roads in Concord, North Carolina. There were no lights at the intersection (Jay's accident caused the traffic department to assess the conditions and place lights here), and traffic was heavy as he waited to cross over.

A fully laden garbage truck weighing sixty thousand pounds was on its way to the landfill when it T-boned Jay's car, pushing it 120 yards and in the process uprooting two trees. There was still enough energy for the truck to flip over and come down on top of his car, crushing it to the size of a shoebox on the right side. The impact was so great it sheered both wheels on the right side off their axles. The entire right side of the car smashed into Jay and shattered every organ in his body.

According to the police officer, the crop of wheat growing on the empty lot on the right-hand side distorted Jay's view. He waited, then took his chance to cross over the intersection, and as he went through the truck hit his car.

Slowly, specifics began to emerge from the accident site. First, there was an emergency response vehicle parked on the opposite side of the road. They were starting up their engine to return to the fire station, and as they prepared to go back, the accident took place right in front of them. They were on the scene before the dust settled. The first responder at Jay's side was a man from First Assembly. God looks after every detail, even in the midst of a crisis.

Jay was listed as a G3, which means no breathing, no pulse, and no visible sign of life. The emergency response crew was phenomenal and had a breathing tube down Jay's throat in seconds. They knew Jay had sustained traumatic injuries, and so they requested a helicopter to take him to the hospital. The road was closed as an ambulance arrived to move Jay from his car to the helicopter. It was very dramatic and all the local television crews were on the scene.

People at the accident site filled us in on some of the particulars. There was a Baptist pastor who phoned people to get them to pray for "the victim." Some of the responders said that there was an amazing calm and a Presence at the accident site. We were not there, so we cannot comment. However, we believe that God was there all the time and that people were sensing His presence.

Jay was being airlifted to a hospital in Charlotte at the same time we were driving to the same venue.

Surgery on Jay's injuries took well over seven hours. Each hour was excruciating as we sat waiting. The doctors had to work on suturing his ruptured lung and then repairing his ruptured aorta. Mortality rates for surgical repair of the aorta are amongst the highest in cardiovascular surgery. The surgery is associated with a high rate of paraplegia because the spinal cord is so sensitive to ischemia (lack of blood supply) and the nerve tissue can be damaged or killed by the lack of blood supply during the surgery. Conservative statistics reveal that 80 to 85 percent of patients die before they get to the hospital. Of those who make it to surgery, approximately 90 percent die within twenty-four hours.

Jay's rib cage was so shattered that they could not do surgery through his chest—they rolled him over and repaired his aorta from the back of his body.

At midnight a weary team of doctor's emerged from the operating theatre and said we could go and see Jay. They reinforced the strong possibility of paraplegia because of lack of blood supply to his spinal cord. I wanted my son to walk again, but more than anything in the world I wanted him to live.

We were all exhausted, but we walked purposefully, hearts filled with anxiety and longing, to the Trauma Intensive-Care Unit where our son was listed as critical. We gowned up and strode down the corridor to where he lay. Pastor Sam walked alongside the three of us. None of us knew what to expect or what we would find; we only knew that he was still breathing and there was still life in his veins.

The tangible silence was broken only by the *whoosh whoosh* of the ventilator that helped Jay to breathe. The monitors around his bed carefully measured the activity of his heart while the pulse oximeter monitored the saturation of oxygen in his blood. He had arterial lines and catheters inserted into him, and as I looked at him, I could hardly believe that this was my son who had walked out the back door twelve hours before, informing me that he loved me "more than life itself!" My heart was broken.

A mere twelve hours before, the sun shone and our world was right-side up. We were all going about our day and planning to eat barbecued salmon on our deck that evening. Instead we were sitting listening to the *whirr* of machines and watching the monitor of the ventilator that kept our son alive.

This day had ended in a way I could never have imagined. I can still recall the dreaded fear and horror that seemed to envelop me. There was nothing I could do, nowhere I could run, no place that was safe.

I felt desperate to touch Jay and hold him, but there was no part of his body that was not injured. There were tubes in his side, and worst of all was the ventilator that blew air into his lungs to keep him alive. I found a small spot above his hand and I bent down and kissed it over and over. I wanted him to feel my love!

Paul was standing next to him and speaking gently. I heard him whisper, "Jay, we love you, son!" What else do you say at such a desperate moment?

Anna sat at the edge of Jay's bed for fear that she might pass out. Her eyes were bloodshot from crying and despair had drained her body dry. Our neatly organized world had been turned upside down and inside out. We knew that it would never be quite the same again.

Paul and Anna drove back to our home in Concord to get some personal items for us because we would be spending the next forty-eight hours at the hospital to be close to Jay. He was in such a critical state that the medical staff felt we needed to be on site.

Paul rummaged through my drawers and closet and gathered some of my belongings. Anna turned off the coffee pot that had sat brewing for the past twelve hours and placed the salmon that had been thawing on the sink back in the refrigerator. She then hurried back upstairs to gather some of her personal items as Paul placed our belongings in a bag.

As Paul got ready to leave our home and head back to the hospital, he looked down the passage for Anna and could not find her. He peered into her bedroom and did not see her there. And then he looked to his left and caught a glimpse of Anna's silhouette. She was down on her knees at her brother's closet with her hands in his sneakers. Paul heard her quavering voice pleading, "Jesus, please let my brother walk in these shoes again."

His heart was shattered. To watch his son fighting for his life in a trauma ward and then to see his daughter's heart broken and aching for her brother was almost more than he could bear. Hot tears spilled down his face in a relentless flow.

Back at the hospital, we learned that Jay's massive internal injuries had caused profuse internal bleeding. His body was double the size from all the saline solution that had been pumped into him to keep him alive. The male nurse on duty told us that in his entire career he had never given any patient more blood.

In the first thirty hours after the accident Jay received forty-two units of blood, plus platelets and plasma. Jay took as much blood as an organ transplant patient would. The concern was that Jay's body would reject the blood and make it nigh on impossible for him to fight this battle.

On Wednesday morning, July 3, we went up at five a.m. to visit Jay. A nurse, observably weary, her face taut with concern, eyes red with fatigue, came to the door and in a worry-laced voice whispered, "We are having some challenges with Jay, so you won't be able to see him."

My heart gave a dull thud in my chest. Fear struck again. In those dreadful hours it would suddenly latch onto me and cling to me like a heavy cloud—foggy, cold, grey, and diffusing into every part of my body. It would creep up my thighs, enter the depth of my stomach, and then fill my mouth with its metallic taste. My parched salivary glands left my tongue feeling like sandpaper as it clung to the roof of my mouth. I would feel my heart pounding in my chest as my hands trembled with a ferocity that alarmed Paul.

Perhaps you are reading this story and wondering how fear can have a place alongside faith. Such questions are difficult to answer. I was praying with absolute sincerity and intensity that God would give us our son back, but I felt my humanity in ways I have never felt it before. I would be less than honest if I did not share the force of my fear, desperation, and agony as I walked through that experience.

We did not comprehend the seriousness of the situation as Jay's vital signs deteriorated rapidly in the early hours of Wednesday morning. His bed sat closest to the nurses' station so that they could monitor him continuously.

The staff in Trauma ICU were so concerned about Jay that they phoned our pastor to let him know they thought they were losing Jay and that he should come and support us through our grief. Within the hour, two van loads of pastors and staff members from First Assembly arrived at the hospital to pray with us.

We went in to the serene little chapel in the hospital complex and prayed and wept for hours. I am thankful we were not aware then that the staff at the hospital had phoned our pastor to inform him of the seriousness of Jay's condition.

On the fourth day, they repaired a deep gash just below Jay's left eye and a gaping wound under his nose where it had hit the steering wheel. We asked why they were only repairing those injuries on the fourth day, and their simple reply was, "We didn't think Jay would survive for more than twenty-four hours."

There were times in the week that followed that I felt waves of desperation and exhaustion overtake me and threaten to engulf me. Fear—cold and slimy—would fight me even in my sleep.

I dreamed one night that an algae-infested pool was pulling me down into its murky depths. I was challenging it as it fought to take me down, pulling me, forcing me, enticing me, down, down, down! I was sinking in its murky mire, my strength sapped, when suddenly a Hand came under me. Gentle, strong, and loving, it bore me safely to the surface.

My rest was always light and fitful, but even in sleep God ministered to me.

Every morning Paul would wake at five a.m. and call the hospital to see how Jay was doing. I could never bring myself to listen to that phone call. I always asked him to close the door so that I did not have to hear the anxiety in his voice. He would always come directly upstairs when the call was completed; he would bend down and kiss me on the cheek and then fill me in on the details. I could hear my heart hammering inside my chest while he updated me. Sometimes the pounding subsided when the news was good. Other times the icy hand of fear would push me out of bed as Paul's voice, threaded with anxiety, revealed another challenge.

My brother, Geoff, flew in from South Africa to support us. He had always been very close to both of our children, and news of Jay's accident had made him hastily change his plans for further missionary travel in India to come directly to Charlotte. We were so thankful for his support.

Friends from all around the world rallied around us in a display of support and love that engulfed us.

The week progressed with ups and downs. By the ninth day Jay's condition seemed to be spiraling downward. My journal recounts that people were phoning us from across the globe, others were praying more fervently, and some gave us comforting scriptures. When I read my notes again, I realized how God's hand was in each detail and how He upheld us and led people to pray at the right time.

The morning of July 10 was Paul's and my anniversary, but it didn't even figure in our thinking. This was to be one of our worst days yet. The early morning phone call was not good news. My journal tells of Paul coming upstairs, his forehead pleated with anxiety as he relayed what the nurse had told him. "Jay had a tough few hours. They struggled with his respirator all night."

Once again, fear hit me in my solar plexus and I felt my heart thumping inside my chest. This was a feeling I would never become accustomed to—our human frames were not made to live with perpetual pain and horror. The human spirit is strong and can survive so much, but it has its limitations. I was thankful for the support I had when I felt that I could barely make it through the next hour. Somehow I always did, as God's hand graciously upheld me through His caring people.

My journal reminds me of the horror of the day. I wrote, "The nine-thirty a.m. visit is devastating for me. I try, but hot tears just flow in an unrelenting stream."

People all over the world were holding prayer meetings for Jay's healing that day, as he battled a host of complications. We would need all the love and support we could get to see us through.

The doctors were desperately trying to find a drug that would help Jay, and they planned a conference call with other medical practitioners from all over the country to assess whether a new drug that had just been approved by the FDA would work. The drug was a high-tech anti-inflammatory medicine that could assist Jay's body in fighting infection, but there was a risk of bleeding.

I had no peace. I had little medical knowledge, but my heart was perturbed.

Other complications set in. Jay's kidneys were struggling; he had a urinary tract infection and pneumonia. The doctors were doing a series of tests and a CAT scan to assess if there was any bleeding on the brain. They were anxious because when they attempted to take Jay off sedation, his brain seemed to be making no response.

One of the doctors saw my distress—because I was openly sobbing. My journal records that he looked at me and said, "Someone is watching over Jay. Ninety percent of all our patients die from these types of injuries and 10 percent of them die in the first twelve hours! Your son is a miracle!"

The medical profession at the hospital was aware of our deep faith because we prayed openly with Jay at his bedside and shared our faith with everyone.

Usually when one from the medical profession spoke positively—which was a rare occurrence considering Jay's injuries—I soaked in their positive words.

I was like a dry sponge and the slightest bit of hope would seep through my pores and infuse me. But this was a very desperate day, and Jay's life hung in the balance.

I remember walking out of the ward that day and Pastor Sam and his wife, Vicki, and Paul's personal assistant were all waiting outside the trauma ward for us. A fresh spasm of anxiety filled my chest and numbness crept up my legs; I collapsed into the arms of Paul's assistant and sobbed uncontrollably.

My cries came from somewhere deep inside of me that I did not even know existed. I wept until there were no tears left to cry. I was empty. I had never in my life felt so broken.

"Why can't it be me? Why must I watch my son suffer?" I cried.

No parent should ever have to watch their child be slowly, tragically, and painfully deprived of life. My mind was in utter distress. There were times I felt as if the angel of death was ever present, seeking to gnaw away the final slivers of hope.

At six-twenty p.m. we were called up to the Trauma ward to meet the young medical intern who had been caring for Jay. He had been with Jay from the very beginning and was a clever and gifted young doctor. He informed us that the initial tests revealed no bleeding on the brain—a vital piece of information if they were to use this new drug. Bleeding anywhere in his body could have been fatal if he were given the drug.

The doctor felt they needed further testing, and we sat waiting anxiously as they did a CAT scan. At the eight-thirty p.m. visit I could see anxiety spread all over the nurse's face and worry lines etched into his forehead. It was at that point I told Paul I was not going home until we met with the doctor who was the head of the Trauma Society and an incredibly capable surgeon.

The wait was lengthy, but eventually around eleven p.m. we saw him. The doctors had assessed Jay's CAT scan and discovered that there were blood clots around the brain, as well as fluid. This meant that they could not use the new FDA-approved drug. Hence the concern I had felt when they told me about the drug.

The expression of weariness on my face must have morphed into one of utter despair and sadness. The doctor looked at me compassionately. My diary records his words: "You have a miracle . . . I didn't believe we would get Jay off the theatre table on the night of his accident, but here he is fighting. Go home, my dear, and sleep. Put your trust in the One who is looking after Jay. Everyone in this hospital acknowledges that there is a Higher Power that is caring for your boy. Go home and get a good rest."

Wow! That was wise advice from a man who claimed he "was a man of science with no personal faith."

The following day Jay was somewhat improved. However, his cardiovascular surgeon wanted to do an echocardiogram to check on the condition of the injury to his atrium and ensure that the clots on his brain were not from bleeding in the atrium of his heart.

It is amazing how we survive some of the darkest hours of our life. We sat at a cafeteria table at the hospital, surrounded by friends, and my brother, Geoff, began to tell stories of when Jay was a little boy. We all laughed so hard we could not contain ourselves.

I was filled with love for this son of mine. We had always called him "our wobbly man" after the character in the Enid Blyton children's book *Noddy*. The wobbly man had an incredible capacity for wobbling over and getting right up again; he would be knocked over by something or someone, and just as quickly he would be back up again. That typified Jay.

He had not had an easy schooling, and life had thrown a lot of challenges his way. But he always found a way through his problems. When someone struck out at Jay, he would be back up again before you could say *Jack Robinson*.

I have mentioned before that memory is a gift! Even the unhappy memories are often reminders of our humanity, and they make us appreciate where we are today. We sat, remembered, laughed, and cried.

The news from the echocardiogram was not good. The wonderful young doctor doing his internship met with us and, in a professional voice tainted with compassion, informed us, "There are no clots around Jay's heart, but they have found a huge hole."

The doctors were not sure if the cavity in his heart was congenital or if it was a trauma wound. However, they could not repair it until all the bacteria and infection was out of his body. I really wondered how many other injuries would surface. Enough already!

A member from our church in Concord visited us on July 11. He had been to see Jay's car and commented that he could not believe anyone could get out of that wreckage alive. Our insurance agent said that in his entire history in the industry he had never seen a worse wreck. When Paul showed me a photo of the wreckage, I was so shaken I just wept. *How could my son possibly be alive?* was all I could wonder. God was the only plausible answer.

The friend who was visiting us had been able to retrieve Jay's wallet from the wreckage and he was returning it to us. It is amazing how something so small could be so significant and meaningful. Paul took Jay's wallet home and put it under his pillow, and there it remained. Every morning, as soon as we opened our eyes, we would pray for Jay while we held his wallet in our hands. When that was accomplished, our day began.

Our church was amazing. The love and support from the congregation beggared belief. When we left the hospital after our evening visits, there was always someone from the church waiting outside Trauma ICU. They would bid us farewell and then stay at the hospital the entire night, praying right through the long and lonely hours. When we arrived for the morning visits at eight-thirty a.m. they would greet us, tell us how Jay was doing, and then they would return home. I know I have said it before, but the body of Christ is incredible!

Whenever we visited Jay, we would talk to him as though he was conscious, telling him what day it was and where he was. We would assure him of people's prayers and let him know of all the phone calls and e-mails flooding in from around the world. I know my son well and was aware of the details that would trouble him, and so I whispered continuously in his ear, "Jay, you have had an accident. It was *not* your fault and no one else was injured. You are going to be fine, son, Keep fighting!"

July 15, my sister Gaille flew in from Australia. It was wonderful having her and Geoff both there to support us and we enjoyed being together despite the dreadful circumstances. As I read my journal again I am reminded of our deep and meaningful friendships. On July 15, we had phone calls from England, India, Texas, South Africa, and Australia. Our phone seemed permanently attached to Paul's ear.

Churches from South Africa called us during their services and prayed with us over the phone. There was a continuous stream of cards, e-mails, flowers, gift baskets, and meals. God's love was shouting loudly through His people. Honestly, I was so emotionally sapped that I soaked in every bit of devotion showered on us. My thirsty, hungry soul drank deep of God's love expressed so powerfully through His church.

The doctors watched Jay's progress carefully. On Wednesday, July 17, the cardiovascular surgeon said that he was monitoring a pocket of fluid on Jay's right side, but all his blood cultures were looking okay. We trusted and prayed for Jay to hold steady so that he could have his heart surgery to suture up the hole. A further CAT scan was ordered to check the progress on his abdomen and chest.

The doctors had not done much about his ruptured liver and spleen because he was too ill to do further surgery. A torn liver can produce a long list of problems of their own and at one stage they were just going to remove Jay's spleen. If they had removed the spleen, I am certain he would not be here today. Not only does the spleen purify the blood, but also it plays a vital role in the immune function, helping to recognize and attack foreign antibodies and disease. No other organ would be more necessary to Jay's long-term health than his spleen. The doctors might not have been aware of problems farther down the track, but God knew!

The days seemed to blur before me and I felt as if I was on the roller coaster ride of my life—one moment I was up and elated at the smallest sign of good news, the next I was spiraling downward with some new challenge.

Jay's CAT scan revealed that his liver and spleen were both healing, but he had caught the hospital superbugs MRSA and C. Diff. Honestly, there were moments that I wondered if his body could handle one more complication. I recall one of the nurses saying, "Your son is the sickest patient we have ever admitted to this hospital. No person with these injuries ever makes it to the hospital alive." Those words would ring over and over in my head and cause me sleepless hours.

Friday, July 19, was Geoff's last day with us. They had given Jay a tracheotomy earlier in the day by making a small incision in his neck to open a direct airway to his windpipe. He had been on the respirator for so long and they feared further infection. Geoff said good-bye to Jay as the rest of the family gathered at the edge of the bed and chatted to the medical staff around us.

Geoff told us months later that he went up to Jay and said, "Jay, I am leaving tomorrow and I want you to know how much Karen and I love you and will be praying for you." Geoff said he saw Jay's eyes open and then roll back in his head. As we walked out of the hospital, Geoff's eyes were full of tears and he fought emotion. When he got home he said to Karen, "Jay is going to die; there is no way he can live through this!"

Saturday morning, July 20, is a day that will live with me forever. Paul got up and phoned the hospital at the usual time. Barb, a wonderful Christian nurse, who had spent hours with us and with Jay answered the phone. There was sheer elation in her voice as the words spilled happily from her lips: "Jay is awake."

He had opened his eyes and tracked her. She asked him to stick out his tongue and he followed the instruction perfectly. Then, with paraplegia at the forefront of her mind, she asked Jay to wiggle his right toe; once again he cooperated. She then asked him to wiggle the left toe and he did it.

Concerned about him, she said, "Are you hurting, Jay?" He shook his head.

She told us that the entire staff of Trauma ICU were ecstatic and acknowledged that the God of the Alexander family had accomplished this!

When Geoff had been saying his farewell to Jay, it is evident that Jay was trying to respond to his voice. Geoff had played a huge role in our children's lives, especially when they were younger. Both of them had, and still have, a very deep affection and bond with their uncle.

We got to Trauma ICU for the morning visit and my legs could not move quickly enough. I had not seen my son's blue eyes for over twenty days.

As I walked towards his bed the young intern doctor was walking out of a side room. He saw us, and in a moment of spontaneous joy he put both his hands up in the air and smiled gleefully at us. We know he had no personal faith because he had openly acknowledged that to us. But in some measure I think that was his way of acknowledging our amazing, magnificent God.

Our son was alive.

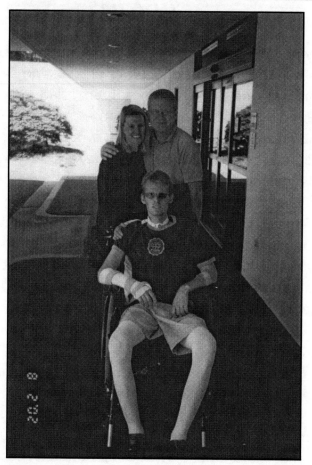

Our first day out of the hospital in August 2002. We were ecstatic, although Jay was still extremely frail.

Reflection

There have been many times in my life that I exercised faith in the midst of difficult or challenging situations. This was one of those times. I reminded myself that I served a great God and I went to His Word for strength and encouragement. Some may wonder how faith and facts can be compatible. I think they are, so let me make a few comments about that.

First, I think that facts are our friends. They are not enemies; they are there to help. The brutal facts stared us in the face on a daily basis in that first month Jay was in Trauma ICU, but on the basis of those facts, the medical profession was able to make some wise decisions that resulted in our son's overall health and well-being. You cannot pray or will the facts away, and you should never ignore them.

When there is a recession, the wisest thing to do is to acknowledge that fact and make decisions on how you can curb your spending. If you are struggling in a relationship, you find meaningful ways of communicating so that the problem is not exacerbated. When you are sick, you go to the doctor so that your symptoms can be attended to. Ignoring your symptoms could aggravate your condition.

Facts help us to make wise and good decisions—so don't ignore them.

Second, I do not think facts nullify faith. Confronting the truth does not imply a lack of faith; it means I have a keen sense of the obvious. I still pray to and believe in God, I still trust Him to hear and answer my prayers, but I play my part by doing what I can to help and to ease the situation. Because I see a doctor when I am sick does not imply I don't trust God for my healing. I believe God can heal my body, but I know that God can use the medical profession to help.

Third, it is my opinion that facts can enhance your faith. In Jay's situation I knew that if God did not answer our prayers Jay would not live. Facing the harsh facts helped me to say, "Only God can accomplish this!" The facts actually enhanced my faith and my prayer life.

Finally, faith does not mean you get everything you pray for. There are countless times God has not answered my prayer in the way I thought He would. At the time I was bitterly disappointed. However, from this perspective, and with a bit more wisdom that has come with age, I can say that God's answer was always right.

It is true there are some things I will never understand. I do not have an answer to some of the problems of life. But as I have grown as a Christ follower, I have realized God is significantly more intelligent than I am; His ways are higher than mine, and above all I can trust Him.

The facts are there to help you. Don't ignore them; use them for your benefit. Once you have faced the facts, place your trust in God and believe He will do what is best. Sometimes facts are brutal. They stare us in the face and they are harsh, but they cannot and should not be ignored, just as faith should never be diminished.

I pray that, despite the facts, your heart will be filled with wild hope!

 *Chapter 12*

Singing Through the Pain and Back Home

Adversity introduces a man to himself.

UNKNOWN

JAY'S EYES, BLUE LIKE THE sky on a cloudless day, warmed my aching heart and filled me with wild hope. Paul, Anna, my sister Gaille and I stood at his bed on Saturday morning, July 20, as Jay looked at us with intensity, responding to our voices. He could not speak with the tracheotomy and respirator, but he mouthed the words "I love you" to each one of us. His eyes were full of pain and sickness, but they were open and he was alive!

When we visited at one-thirty that afternoon, Jay's eyes were sad and appealed to me. He looked at me and mouthed the word, "Mom!" Desperation and pain were engraved in his face and there was nothing that I could do to ease his suffering. He was coughing perpetually and it distressed Anna so much that she had to walk out of the ward. Still, it was a good sign that his lungs were working.

What was touching to all of us was that every time he coughed he tried to bring his hand up to cover his mouth. He couldn't speak, but his eyes were talking. They were looking at me and saying, "Where am I? What am I doing here?" I wished I could take his place, bear his suffering, relieve him of his pain, if only for an hour. But I couldn't, because this was his cross to bear. All that I could do was be there for him and show him how much I loved him.

A nurse came over to us. "Wow, doesn't he look great? He is doing so well!" Everything is relative, and I suppose in comparison to how he had been a few days before, he was looking "great." But his eyes told me a different story.

At the eight-thirty p.m. visit, Jay was trying to tell us something, but we could not understand what he was mouthing. We could sense his frustration, and it seemed he was imploring us not to leave him.

For the first time in over twenty days Anna did not accompany us to the evening visit. Exhaustion had caught up with her and she just needed a few hours of respite. When Jay asked us where his sister was, it was a good sign that his brain was functioning. The clots on his brain had given the doctors some serious concern regarding the future of his mental state, but I could tell that his mind was clear. Miracles were happening before our eyes. I prayed earnestly that night that Jay would have minimal pain.

The next day, when we went to visit Jay, he was alert. I told him he had been in a car accident, and he looked at me and frowned. We could see he was trying to ask a question, and suddenly it dawned on us that he was desperately trying to inquire, "Was anyone else in the car with me?" I quickly added, "No one else was in the car, and nobody else was injured in the accident." He sighed as relief spread across his face.

With his arms stiffly by his side, he began to hit his legs with them; he became quite agitated. I knew immediately what he was anxious to find out. I asked him, "Are you worried that your legs aren't moving?" He nodded. I looked into his eyes and said, "Jay, your legs are fine. You are going to walk again. They are not working because you have been on a paralysis drug that has kept you from moving. You will soon be running again."

He didn't smile, but he closed his eyes briefly and mouthed the words, "Thank you, Lord!"

That evening, as we were leaving the hospital, one of Jay's nurses asked Paul if she could speak to him. He went over to the nurses' station wondering what she wanted. With emotion in her voice she said, "Your family has changed the atmosphere in this ward. There was a lot of tension before y'all came here, but you have brought tranquility and harmony to this place. The doctors and nurses are getting along with each other, and there is a sense of peace here. And our records show that our patients are getting better quicker."

As Christ followers, God's presence goes with us wherever we go, and it always dispels the darkness and brings hope. That is precisely what was happening in the Trauma ICU ward. We could not take the credit for what the Spirit of God was so evidently doing in that sterile ICU unit.

By Monday, July 22, we knew that Jay was on the slow road to recover. The first signs of his humor started to come back—and when someone is so desperately sick, you know that humor is good for the soul. He was smiling and teasing his dad, and it warmed all our hearts. When you have been deprived of any joy, the smallest act or sign of hope can be so invigorating that you feel as if nothing is impossible.

We also knew he was improving because he had the hospital staff running to listen to his requests for tea, juice, milk—all of which were prohibited because he couldn't take anything orally. It didn't stop him from perpetually trying to charm the nurses into giving him the forbidden liquids. They told us frequently that he was their favorite patient.

We were amazed when we heard that the police officer who had given me the news about Jay on that dreadful day had gone with his partner to pay Jay a visit. Evidently, they had also gone looking for us so they could see how we were doing, but we had left the hospital to get a Starbucks, so unfortunately we never saw them.

We were touched when the nurse told us that they had phoned every day to find out how Jay was doing. She said the people from the emergency vehicle who had rescued Jay from the wreckage had also called on a daily basis. We began to find out just how much the community had responded to our plight and how carefully they followed Jay's progress. In a world that can sometimes be harsh and unkind, there are still so many good and caring people. We should never forget that.

One of Jay's nurses, James, who had been with Jay on his first night in ICU, was leaving the ward permanently. We went to him to thank him for nursing our son. With tears in his eyes he said, "Thank you for the privilege to care for your son." It is a humbling experience when people whom you should thank are thanking you.

To this day I have a deep respect for the medical profession, and I will be eternally grateful to all those who assisted our son, from his traumatic surgery through to his recovery. They were compassionate and kind all of the time.

During the weeks that Jay was in the Trauma ward there was only one nurse who was void of empathy. She was often short tempered with patients and was particularly rough when she bathed Jay. One morning we got to Jay and found that this nurse, thoroughly empty of compassion, had tied his arms so tightly to his side that he could not move them. He looked at me and implored, "I beg you, please loosen them!'

I was furious with that woman. However, I was also deeply aware that something of normality was returning to my life and I could feel other emotions. All I had experienced for the past number of weeks was fear and agony of heart and soul. It was almost energizing to feel renewed passion and a feeling of anger that my son had to bear unnecessary discomfort.

That was the only time in ICU that I had a concern about one of the staff. For that particular lady, nursing was simply a way of earning money, not a calling.

But we focused on the positives. Bit by bit the doctors were lowering Jay's morphine intake and weaning him off the respirator. At times he was very anxious and wanted us to stay with him for as long as possible. His entire ribcage was fractured and the pain he endured was severe. Too, the doctors were struggling with his tummy and had to keep putting tubes down his nose, which he inevitably pulled out.

As we reflect, we realize that some of the struggles the doctors were beginning to have with Jay's stomach were the onset of Crohn's, a terrible disease that plagued him for over eight years and more than likely was as a result of his traumatic accident.

On July 29 the staff told us that they were getting ready to move Jay out of Trauma ICU. That was a heartening piece of news. Jay had only been off the critical list for a week but was still listed as "serious."

At our five p.m. visit we had to try and move Jay in his bed because he was uncomfortable and wanted to be stretched. I went behind him and for the first time saw the surgery scars on his back. I was aghast! He had two large scars and they were not pretty.

As the fluids he'd retained emptied out of Jay, he became emaciated and all his bones stuck out of his paper-thin flesh. He looked like a malnourished person from a concentration camp. But even though he looked awful, the nurses assured us he was doing well. And although he still could not eat anything or drink fluids, that did not stop him from asking. He asked the staff if he could shower, take a walk, drink tea, and eat fruit, all to no avail. He would constantly try and get the staff to give in to his requests by suggesting if they did something for him, he would sit up longer or would try harder with his physio. To his chagrin nothing seemed to work. But he did add color to their day and made a seemingly dismal place a little more cheerful with his quirkiness. They found him charming and engaging and suggested that he should work for the CIA when he got better because he was a skilled negotiator.

On Tuesday, July 30, as we arrived for our morning visit, Jay was being wheeled out of Trauma ICU. As he was escorted out of the ward, the nurses and doctors stood around him and applauded. One of the nurses said cheerfully to Paul, "I have always prayed that I would see one miracle during my nursing career. Now I have seen one. Thank you for allowing me to share my first ever miracle with you!"

Another nurse told us enthusiastically, "The morning that Jay opened his eyes for the first time, it was only two a.m., but all the staff on duty that morning gathered around Jay's bed and there was not a dry eye there."

Remember, this was a Trauma ward where the sickest and most injured patients came. This was the ward where gunshot victims arrived, where brain injuries were prevalent, where desperately sick people came and many of them died. It was not a place for the faint hearted. Yet the staff had all witnessed an incredible miracle and it touched their lives in a profound way.

Jay was placed in a Progressive Care ward. It was horrible. He shared it with three sick old men, and the atmosphere was not conducive to his recovery. It was constantly noisy, which didn't allow for good rest, and it smelled obnoxious, as the elderly patients relieved themselves in their beds.

We realized just how fragile and weak Jay was when they decided to let him sit in a chair and it took forty-five minutes to get him from the bed to the chair. When he stood, it was only for a few short seconds before he was panting and out of breath.

One day, we watched as his physiotherapist worked with him. I was in tears watching my once strapping, handsome lad reduced to skin and bone, unable to do anything unaided. I had to remind myself that it was okay, that a sixty-thousand-pound truck going sixty miles an hour had hit him and it would take time to recover.

Once Jay was off the respirator and could talk again, we phoned my parents. It had been an incredibly anxious time for both of them. Living in Australia and waiting for news on a daily basis was at times agonizing. They had lived through the moments of fear and terror with us and were thrilled when Jay moved out of Trauma ICU.

My parents were not aware, however, that Jay had started talking again, and so we phoned them to surprise them. My mom's familiar voice answered the phone after a few rings, "Hello, hello?" And then she heard Jay's faltering voice reply, "Hello!" She wept uncontrollably. Tears were rolling down Jay's face, spilling down his neck and wetting his hospital gown. It was a tender and precious moment as his grandparents clung to every word he spoke, fully aware that the sound waves being transmitted over thousands of miles were a miracle in more ways than one.

Tears were a common occurrence during that phase of Jay's recovery. When he heard that his Uncle Geoff had flown in and spent two weeks at his bedside, hot, salty tears poured down his cheeks once again. He would often look at Paul and me and thank us for being his parents, and then he would cry.

We understood that some of his emotion was also the effect of the drugs. He said many kind and wonderful things to us-—and there are times now I wish I could dose his tea with a bit of morphine to evoke some of that emotion! No, in all truth, Jay has always shown his love and appreciation for his family and I am sure the accident played no small part in his gratitude quotient.

Aside from the emotions, Jay's thoughts were sometimes muddled and confused. He always knew what day it was and where he was, but he would sometimes worry us with the things he said. We were assured that this too came from all the drugs and the weeks of being unconscious.

While his recovery advanced, his nurse in the Progressive Care ward had none of the graces that the staff had constantly displayed in the Trauma ward. She kept asking him in the crudest of ways if he needed the bedpan. Jason was unimpressed; sick as he was, he was not a child and did not appreciate her undignified manner.

One day, as his nurse was examining Jay, she casually lifted his gown up in front of all of us. I wanted to slap her. When someone is sick, his or her dignity still needs to be preserved. I felt inclined to suggest to the hospital manager that this particular nurse go and do a refresher course in patient care, but I never did. I was never more pleased than when Jay was moved from that ward into a private room on his own.

The hospital staff began to prepare us for the long road to recovery and told us to anticipate Jay being in the Rehabilitation ward for up to a year. I was just happy to have my son and was determined that we would sing through the rain and through the pain, but we would eventually get our son home.

When a bed freed up for Jay in the Rehab ward, my stomach flipped with joy and we all accompanied him there as he was wheeled out on a stretcher. The morning air was sweltering, and beads of perspiration gathered on Jay's forehead, but it was wonderful for him to feel the warmth of the sun after the cold and sterile air of the hospital.

I was upset, however, when I discovered that Jay was transferred to the brain-injury section of the Rehab ward. He was placed next to a severely brain-damaged man who screeched and wailed. It was emotionally distressing, and for someone vulnerable at every level it was of concern to me. I knew that Jay would never recover in a noisy ward like that.

I went to see a nurse. "My son does not have brain damage. Please, could you remove him from this ward and find him a more suitable one." Enunciating each word with precision, she regretfully informed me, "Your son has been unconscious for three weeks, my dear. For us that constitutes a brain injury. We are not saying that your son has any permanent brain damage. However, he does have an injury to his brain, which we believe in time will heal."

I was realizing afresh just how traumatic Jay's injuries really were. He was still a susceptible and ailing patient who needed consistent medical care. However, they were happy to grant me my request, and they promptly removed Jay from the noisy ward to a private one, although still in the brain-injury section of Rehab.

Within a day they discovered that Jay had a further injury. He had a severely broken arm that they had been unaware of in the Trauma ward. Fortunately, this was the last injury we were to discover. I am not sure I could have handled too much more.

They were able to get Jay in for surgery and put in a steel pin to repair his arm. Before Jay went in for surgery, he said to the surgeon, "Doctor, when the cast is removed from my arm, will I be able to play the piano?"

The doctor looked at him with a quiet assurance and said, "Of course you will."

To which Jay replied, "Ah, good, because I couldn't play the piano before!"

The staff was caught off guard by Jay's humor and antics. His physiotherapist said, "We don't see much humor in this ward; people are too sick. Your son is a rare specimen." Indeed he was—he shouldn't even have been there! But he was and he was determined to sing through the pain.

After ten days in the Rehab ward Jay was beginning to pine for home. They kept telling him he could go home when he ate all of the food on his plate. Hospital food was unpalatable at the best of times, and Jay didn't have much of an appetite. But we were so anxious to get him home that Paul would sometimes finish the food and the staff would report, "A clean plate!"

When Jay was able to get out of bed in ten minutes with assistance, we knew he was on the road to recovery. His negotiation skills were in constant use in the rehab ward. He was on a heavy drug for his MRSA and C. Diff, and it meant constant injections. He also had to have injections directly into his tummy to keep his blood thin.

Jay constantly tried to negotiate with the nurses and bribe them to come back later, or to give a double dose of the injection the following day and leave him in peace for one more day—anything to delay the inevitable and avoid the constant prodding and pricking of needles. To his chagrin, it never worked. But it did put a smile on their faces, which was a rare sight in the Rehabilitation ward of the hospital.

One day Paul sat watching the staff trying to administer another injection into Jay's veins. His veins had all collapsed from the constant use of intravenous needles. The exhaustion and pain carved on Jay's face as they prodded and pricked was more than Paul could bear, and he cried out, "Stop! No more—you are not going to hurt my son anymore!" It was out of character for Paul, the family optimist with the perpetual smile on his face and the constant spring in his step. But he had simply had enough.

Seeing your child suffer is one of the most excruciating types of agony a parent can experience. It had finally reached its limit, and Paul could not bear watching Jay hurt for one more minute.

They stopped immediately, but informed us that giving Jay the drug orally would cost us twelve hundred dollars a month. We didn't care; we would find the money somehow, but we could not watch Jay suffer another moment.

Jay worked hard in the rehabilitation hospital. He had a positive attitude and he always managed a smile—singing through the pain. Sweat would glisten on his brow as he struggled to walk again and do the most basic of exercises. He would get back to his ward, and as his heart rate slowed down and his body settled, he would start shivering and the hairs on his body would stand up straight as goose bumps covered his weary frame.

Jay was determined to do thirty steps a day so that he could go home. The nurses could only stop the injections into his stomach when he was walking sufficiently to keep the blood moving around his body. If he was to go home, he needed to walk so that the injections could cease. He was highly motivated.

And it paid off. On Wednesday, August 14, Paul signed all the papers for Jay to be released from the hospital. He was going home!

The day began like any other. Nurses and doctors moved in purposeful strides up and down the corridors checking on their patients. Parents in various stages of emotion walked through the passages. Some were filled with anxiety and others had smiles that stretched across their faces, knowing their loved one was on the road to recovery.

An orderly in brightly colored scrubs helped Jay to get dressed, and then he had a full round of visits from various white-coated doctors. We received instructions from them about Jay's care and an abundance of painkillers to ease the journey to recovery.

We were ready and happy to leave the hospital for the final time, and the nurse called for a wheelchair to take Jay to the car. We waited for over an hour . . . and no wheelchair arrived. We rang for the nurse and were told that for some reason they were struggling to locate a wheelchair.

"What? You can't find a wheelchair in a rehab ward?" I said with astonishment to Paul.

After waiting for another half an hour Paul looked at Jay and with deep concern asked him, "Do you think if Mom and I assist you, that you could try to walk to the door?" It wasn't far, but Jay's lung capacity was seriously diminished and he still had little strength. Every step for him was a struggle, and when he walked just thirty paces he panted as if he had run a marathon.

He responded with his usual optimism, "Yes, I can do it!"

We put a belt around him that he used for physiotherapy, and then I took his left arm and Paul clutched his right one, and slowly we walked down the corridor to the front door. We may have been dragging our feet, but our hearts were racing with sheer delight at the thought of taking our son home. Step by painful step, Jay moved each foot like a weary tortoise and then waited while Paul went to the car and opened the door for him.

I do think we experience internal seasons of the soul. I had gone through the most treacherous of winters. But as we slowly and carefully lowered Jay onto the front seat of the car, I knew the winter of my soul had passed and spring had arrived in one rapturous moment filled with wild hope.

Jay maneuvered his body while Paul gently took his legs and moved them across, placing them cautiously onto the floor. As Paul glanced down, he realized that Jay was wearing the shoes his sister had placed her hands in on that dismal Monday night of July 1, when she cried out, "Jesus, let my brother walk in these shoes again!"

He looked up, tears brimming in his eyes.

And then I recalled how Anna had placed her hands on my shoulder and said, "Mommy, my brother will walk out of this hospital!" That is why the staff could not find a wheelchair that day. God was fulfilling His promise to us that our precious son would "walk out of this hospital."

The sun was shining with a radiance that seemed to warm us internally and I had never seen the sky look so blue as every cloud vanished. Jay could walk.

Everything seemed right with the world!

Reflection

At the time of this writing Jay's accident was twelve years ago when he was twenty-two years old. This has not been an easy chapter to write. Details have flooded back, but with them have come moments of deep gratitude. Writing has ripped the scab off a memory that I didn't want to recall. However, in many ways writing and remembering has been cathartic for me.

I have said it before, but it bears repeating: memory is a gift. An extraordinary gift. It is my capacity for memory that enables me to make wise decisions about today and tomorrow. As I look back, I remember the good and the bad, and even those sad and painful memories are helpful for me. The happy memories fill me with warmth and the painful ones remind me of how much the human spirit can endure. Painful memories also remind me of my humanity and of how my God walked with me through the darkest night.

What did we as a family take from this experience? How has this ordeal changed our lives? Well, joy and thankfulness are close companions that flow through our family DNA. Our lives have changed because we are aware that life is short. It is a gift.

Our days are numbered, and truth be told, none of us know when our time will come to breathe our final breath. And so it is that as a family we value each moment we have with each other. We don't think you can ever say "I love you!" enough. Spending reckless moments of time with each other, drinking copious amounts of tea, and belly laughing over meals is part of our joyous response to our memory of lament. Each and every precious moment with each other is a gift so extraordinary and beautiful that somehow there will always be echoes of joy emanating from the remnants of deep and abiding pain.

In the midst of it all, our amazing God upheld us through each moment. We felt His tender love and care expressed through His people. His sorrow was evidenced through so many individuals who traveled from afar to weep and pray with us. Thousands of friends around the world joined us in our journey of lament and upheld us with their prayers. God's love rang loud and clear through the body of Christ.

And now we live with the echoes of eternity and the realization that when life on earth is over, it will just be beginning. Therein is the fusion of sadness and joy all wrapped up in the promise of hope after life. These are the echoes of joy that emanate from our past grief.

If your heart is aching and you wonder if you will ever smile again, be assured that the darkness will pass and the sun will shine again. There were times that the hurting in my heart was so intense I begged God to give me relief, even if for just a moment.

Pain is not a normal state. But I would never have known the anguish of pain for my son if I had not experienced the intense love I had for him. It is because I loved so deeply that I grieved so profoundly. And in that sense, pain is a gift. Can you imagine not feeling pain when there is loss? My pain exposes my humanity and my capacity to love. And as a family we learned that you can still sing through the pain.

Your pain will heal and be replaced by a deeper and more profound ability to love and to give to others. Allow your heart to fill with wild hope!

 Chapter 13

Discovering Beauty Through Pain in England

Since love grows within you, so beauty
grows. For love is the beauty of the soul.

ST. AUGUSTINE

WE ARRIVED HOME IN CONCORD to a huge "Welcome Home, Jay" banner plastered above the garage doors. The first order of the day was to get Jay inside and make him his long-awaited cup of tea. His hands were too shaky and weak to hold a cup, so his sister sat next to him and carefully placed the cup to his lips as he drank what he called "the nectar of the gods." His eyes seemed hungry as he took in his surroundings—it was almost as if he was seeing some things for the first time.

I looked at Jay for a very long time. I sat and watched my Anna as she patiently and tenderly waited for her brother to finish his tea sip by sip. I wondered about the impact of the trauma on all of our lives. Only time would tell. But right at that moment we were all together. I knew then that I would never stop hugging them, telling them how much I loved them, and savoring every single moment that God allowed us to share together on this earth. I had a perspective on life that can only be garnered by "walking through the fire."

Eventually the MRSA bacteria that was invading Jay's bloodstream was brought under control, which enabled the doctor's to repair the hole in his heart. After the surgery we saw Jay's recovery speed up. Day by day, his lung capacity increased as he walked farther and farther. We loved watching his remarkable zest for life and his sheer determination to bounce back.

One of the remarkable miracles for me was that Jay experienced very little pain during his recovery time. In fact, we never used any of the painkillers Jay received when he left the Rehabilitation ward. With every rib broken in his body, the doctors thought that Jay would have a painful road ahead of him. However, I had prayed persistently that God would help Jay with the pain and that prayer was answered.

I was aware how completely God had met my request a few weeks later. Jay had developed an excruciatingly sore ingrown toenail, which worsened as the week progressed. Eventually it was so torturous that he took one of the painkillers to help relieve the discomfort. We all realized what a miracle it was that he had never had to use that medication up until that point.

Jay had only been home a couple of weeks when Paul had to fulfill a commitment in England. I was anxious about being alone with Jay, but Paul had already canceled many speaking engagements, and we felt it was necessary for him to accomplish this particular one. We had no idea that the outcome of this trip would effect a whole new direction in our lives.

Cutting out a lot of detail, the UK visit resulted in an invite to take on the leadership of Mattersey Hall College. I have to be honest and admit that the thought of going there did not appeal to me in the slightest. Paul had a burden for Europe and could see all the possibilities that this position could afford him in fulfilling his passion.

But I had vivid and unhappy memories of our previous time in the UK and of the unkind manner in which we were treated. I told Paul that I did not want to give the slightest consideration to this possibility. I pushed the thought and potential of going to England back with the strength of a lion, determined that nothing would change my mind. However, Paul gently nudged me to pray about the invitation and seek God's will.

I am grateful that my husband is not an arrogant or forceful man and that he has never considered that being the head of our home empowers him to have his way irrespective of those he loves. One of his deep convictions is that every new opportunity or calling that he receives needs to be validated by every member of his family. He is convinced that the children and I are an intrinsic part of his life and ministry, which implies that God would not call him without calling all four of us. And so I prayed . . . earnestly!

To my utter astonishment—and I must emphasize both words—God affirmed the call in my heart and placed a burden in me to go and serve His kingdom in that part of the world.

Although Jay was well on the road to recovery, he was still vulnerable in many ways. As I mentioned previously, he had started to display the first symptoms of Crohn's disease. It was a difficult decision for me to leave him and entrust him to the care of my heavenly Father. I would have to learn to cast my cares on the Lord with great frequency as Jay faced some challenging moments with his disease.

We had lived in the States for four years and our children did not have another relative living on this continent. It was a difficult time for Anna as she navigated her way in prayer and eventually came to peace with our calling. Jay is the pragmatic member of our family and encouraged us wholeheartedly to take up the challenge of this new position.

And so, in July 2004 we packed up once again and made the trip across the Atlantic to take up our new post.

Our years in England were filled with excitement and vision. We saw tremendous growth as men and women came from all over the world to study at Mattersey Hall College and Graduate School.

Paul was passionate about the graduate program, and he and the team grew it from one master's degree to five, as well as a doctor of ministry and PhD program. The growth was phenomenal and impacted many students across the world.

Paul's approach was innovative and attracted a lot of attention. He negotiated with the validating university to offer a course taught through a number of intensives that were specifically designed to help people in leadership.

He delighted as he saw many mature leaders grow and develop their theological and leadership skills. It was not uncommon to have student cohorts where people literally flew in from around the world to participate in a weekend of teaching.

Perhaps our most significant achievement at Mattersey Hall was the introduction of required mission trips as part of the undergraduate program. Paul has always been somewhat idealistic and was convinced that practical training should parallel the academic process. He had two ideals that to him were non-negotiable. The first was that all students, in each year of their studies, should be committed to a mission trip somewhere in the world. The second was that each member of faculty should be equally as involved and would lead these trips.

Over the years teams scattered annually to many different countries. Mattersey students scrubbed dirty hospital wards in Russia. Building projects in Romania were helped along and orphans in South Africa were fed. Teams traveled to Jordan, France, Sri Lanka, Thailand, Central Africa, and many other places. Our students served some impoverished parts of British cities as well, and it was thrilling to see people led to Christ on almost a daily basis in these needy communities.

As we reflected on these initiatives, it was wonderful to hear story after story of students' lives being lastingly impacted by the Mattersey missions trips. In fact, we heard many students declare that the single biggest reason why they chose to study with us was because of the commitment that we had to global mission.

It was during our first year in England that Anna married Rich. Three years later they blessed us with our first grandbaby, a little girl called Ava. She crept into our hearts and we fell in love with her the moment we laid eyes on her. Tylan followed eighteen months later. He has given us countless hours of joy with his charming personality and wonderful sense of humor. It is no exaggeration to say that the two of them have colored our world.

All of this excitement at Mattersey and in our family was interrupted by a shocking discovery. Before leaving the United States Paul received a letter informing him that he was entitled to a free annual medical checkup. He was feeling fit and healthy, and so he pushed the letter to the side of his desk, choosing to ignore it. The problem was that as I was dusting and clearing his workstation the following day, I happened to discover the infamous piece of paper.

I immediately challenged Paul to go and have his annual medical exam. He emphatically refused to do so, declaring his impeccable health by dropping to the ground and performing twenty push-ups. I was totally unimpressed with his efforts and informed him in no uncertain way that if he loved his children and me, he would go for his check up. He looked at me aghast and affirmed his undying love for all of us.

I was reassured by his words but insisted that he prove his commitment to us by picking up the phone and making the dreaded appointment. He muttered and mumbled and then, with a huge sigh of resignation and defeat, he picked up the phone to call the doctor's office to set up the consultation.

I sat right there in front of him and waited to ensure the appointment was made before leaving his study. Yes, I can be stubborn, but I love my husband and wanted to ensure that he did due diligence with his health so that he could live to see his children marry and have grandchildren. I also had my own personal desire to live with him into our old age.

The visit to the doctor was largely uneventful except for the discovery of a bicuspid aortic heart valve. It is a congenital condition that occurs in 1 to 2 percent of the population. The doctor explained to Paul that two of the aortic valvular leaflets fused during development, resulting in a bicuspid as opposed to a tricuspid configuration. He did tell Paul that he wanted to do further testing.

When we arrived in the UK, Paul found a good doctor and went to see him to ensure that he understood his condition. Thus began a long and drawn-out saga of nearly three years. Test after test and delay after delay ultimately revealed a large aneurism on Paul's rising aorta.

The doctor that performed the transesophageal echocardiogram told Paul that if Paul had any pain he would not release him from the hospital because the dilation was so large. Paul was entirely without pain but was told not to exert himself in any way. The processes in the British health system resulted in long delays between visits to medical specialists. As a result it was ten long months before Paul was finally admitted for surgery.

The wait was an agonizing time for me personally. We were made aware of the seriousness of Paul's condition and he was encouraged to slow down. Unfortunately, Paul has no understanding of the words "slow down," and so his pace continued with the same ferocity and passion he had always displayed.

There were times in the quiet blackness of the night that I could not hear him breathing. In my panic I would place my hand firmly on his back and leave it there until I felt his frame move rhythmically up and down as he inhaled and exhaled the air around him. It often left me with my heart pounding in my chest and a prayer going heavenward that God would spare him for many more years ahead.

Paul confessed to me later that he would regularly cry out at night to the Lord and beseech Him, "Please, let me live so that I can serve You and see my family grow." He appealed to the Lord to give him enough years to see grandchildren born to the two of us.

On July 18, 2007, Paul was admitted to Sheffield Northern General for an aortic valve and root replacement. I remember driving him to the hospital on the day before his surgery.

Our children had flown in from the States to support us during the ordeal. We drove past green fields filled with yellow delight as sunflowers sprouted their loveliness all along the way. I thought of what lay ahead, and for a fleeting moment the thought crossed my mind, *Is this the last time the three of us will drive with Paul?* But I pushed that quickly aside and tried to concentrate on getting through the day and breathing in the beauty of the countryside. It was not easy.

I recall the moment was almost surreal as I listened to the doctor's words: "There are risks with this surgery . . . Your husband can die . . .

We have to inform you of the possibility of brain damage." The doctor explained in his monotone voice, emphasizing each word as he spat them out, that the challenge with Paul's surgery was that his aneurism went past the junction to the carotid artery to his brain, which was why there was a high risk of brain damage.

I remained calm on the outside while the words spun around my brain, tormenting me mercilessly. I felt my insides shaking and despite all Paul's positive and reaffirming words that he had no intention of dying, I was afraid. "Please, please, please, God, don't let Paul die," I implored the Lord with an earnestness that came somewhere from the depth of my inner being.

There are times in our lives when we are confronted with harsh realities. We wish we could run or hide from them, but we know we can't. The day of surgery arrived. Fifteen hours was designated for Paul's surgery. The surgeon spoke emphatically, "This is a big one. In fact, after a heart transplant, this is the most invasive surgery we do." It was as if each syllable he uttered was like a heavy weight that thickened the air.

The surgeon knew his words appalled me and yet did nothing to comfort me. But what distressed me most was when he told us that they'd place Paul in ice and then "turn him off," while they replaced his aortic valve and cut out the aneurism, replacing it with a prosthetic aorta. I remember Paul asking with a worry-laced voice, "What do you mean by 'turn me off'?"

Unable or unwilling to meet Paul's gaze, the doctor fumbled for words. "Well, let me see . . . we . . . um . . ."

Paul, realizing the surgeon was struggling to find the appropriate words, said, "You mean you kill me!"

The doctor smiled back at Paul and in a voice of resignation replied, "That is one way of putting it." His flippancy, tinged with a hint of joviality, did nothing to impress me because personally I did not see the humor in the moment.

Only when Paul was safely ensconced in his bed, covered with starched white sheets and layers of grey blankets, did I feel I could leave him. As I exited his ward, a fresh spasm of anxiety filled my chest and I reluctantly made my way to my empty room to while away the long, dark hours.

I was up most of the night before surgery. The doctor's words echoed in my mind, plaguing me through the lonely night. The thought of death would suddenly hit me like a slap on the face and trouble my weary brain. The power of the doctor's words were like a hammer beating slowly and steadily in my head, striving to drive out any sense of hope. The night was long, and I tossed and turned as sleep evaded my weary frame.

As soon as the sun poked through the blinds of my grey hospital room, the memory of the nightmare ahead of me jolted me out of my bed. I went hastily down to Paul's ward. Recollections of Jay's all too familiar ward with its cold, sterile atmosphere, threatened to demoralize me.

Paul was sleepy from the tablets he had been given the night before, but he smiled when he saw me and I could sense he was trying to drive the sadness from my aching heart.

My eyes were red from lack of sleep and I knew that Paul was aware of the heaviness that enshrouded me. We held hands tightly and prayed together. He asked God to give Anna, Jay, and me strength through the hours that lay ahead, and I asked Jesus to guide the surgeon's hands.

As they wheeled Paul to the operating theatre, I walked alongside him and then kissed him good-bye at the door. My eyes did not leave him until he was out of sight. The intensity of my emotion made my vocal chords numb, and the pain in the back of my throat intensified as I swallowed back the tears that threatened to overwhelm me. Never have I felt so alone or frightened.

Geoff and his wife, Karen, were also in the UK to support us through this time. We all sat and waited hour after excruciating hour. After eight hours of agony, we got a call informing us that surgery was over and I could go and see Paul. I raced up to ICU with my brother by my side.

It is amazing how sometimes a smell or a place will suddenly lift the lid off your memory bin and out will leap a thought shocking you with its crystal-clear recollection. When I got to the door I could not enter ICU. I froze. I felt waves of nausea wash over me; my legs were wobbly and my heart pounded with such rapidity that I thought it would beat right out of my chest. Suddenly, billows of memory rolled over me as I recalled the trauma of Jay's accident some five years before.

The sterile walls, white-coated doctors, nurses in their scrubs, people in varying stages of grief, all closed in on me as the antiseptic odor, like a noxious cloud, hit my nostrils, stifling me.

I stood as blackness engulfed me . . . and then it was quiet. Only seconds had passed but it seemed like hours. My brother's voice penetrated the roaring silence, and his words brought me back to consciousness.

"Cam, are you all right?"

I breathed deeply, gathered myself together, and walked slowly and deliberately into the ICU ward to see Paul. As I paced down the corridor, the heavy atmosphere—infused with an antiseptic smell and the sounds of hissing machines—hit me with a depressing blow. But I knew I had to be strong.

I walked up to Paul's bed and saw his face was whiter than a cloud on a summer day. I had never seen him look so pale before. In a moment of silliness, I asked the nurse if she had put baby powder on Paul's face. She smiled and said, "Do you honestly think we have nothing better to do than rub powder on our patients' faces?" I felt really stupid!

I sat beside Paul's bed, and tears rolled down my cheeks. I couldn't stop crying. He looked so weak and sick lying there with a breathing tube down his throat as the ventilator worked to assist his lungs. In all the years I had known Paul and been married to him, I had never seen him look so frail and vulnerable, and it frightened me.

The little nurse caring for Paul had milky eyes and wore a sweet, dimpled smile. I sat mute and paralyzed as I listened to her relay the details of Paul's surgery. She looked at me with empathy and said, "You've never been in an ICU ward before have you?"

My vocal chords betrayed my sheer exhaustion and emotion as I told her that I had sat in an all too familiar Trauma ICU ward for twenty-eight days with my son, but I was not alone then because Paul and I went through that crisis together.

Tears prickled the corners of my eyes, and despite me biting my cheek I was not able to stop the flow as I looked at Paul. I felt a wrench in my heart for the man I loved so much and could not imagine living my life without. I was going through this crisis without him by my side to strengthen me.

Our children were an incredible support and comfort to me, but there is nothing as lonely as journeying through a trial without your spouse to support you. It felt as if my soul had been through winter one too many times. I sat there quietly, and with a plea that came from the deepest part of me, I cried, "Lord! Please spare me from sitting in an ICU ward one more time!"

Eight days later, and after some complications, Paul was released from the hospital. He had spent four days in the ICU ward and another four in a general ward. When the doctors were able to stabilize him after complications with his kidneys, he made steady progress. He was weak, frail, scarred and vulnerable. But he was alive. I saw beauty in a way I had not seen it before.

There can be something truly lovely about imperfection and brokenness. I had never perceived that before this moment. I suddenly realized that the marred and imperfect vessel can have a beauty all of its own. Beneath the ugly, painful scar of Paul's surgery was beauty—he was alive. His body would bear scars forever, but underneath the wrapping of pain and brokenness was the allure of his strength and courage.

As we left the hospital and the brisk fresh English air hit him, a smile spread across his face and tears welled in his eyes. *Wild hope* flooded through his veins. He was alive. And above all of that was the spectacular opportunity of another day to live together, the chance to sit and watch another sunrise and enjoy the magnificent world God had created. We could dream of grandchildren and many more years to serve Jesus together. What an incredible gift.

Anna and Jay were a wonderful support to us throughout our time in the UK and especially through the difficult days of Paul's surgery.

Reflection

That was seven years ago. I don't take one day of my life for granted. Every single day is a gift for me—an amazing treasure to live with the man I have loved since I was sixteen years old. I never get tired of saying "Thank you!" to Jesus for sparing his life.

At times we look for beauty in all the wrong places. But beauty goes much deeper than the skin. Sometimes beauty can surprise us because it is wrapped in a way that we could never anticipate. Most of us love pretty wrappings, but many times what lies beneath is not beautiful at all. However, under the sometimes ugly layers of pain and brokenness you can discover pure, unadulterated beauty.

As human beings we can sometimes be fickle. I think how sad it is when a person gets tired of their spouse because their body is no longer youthful and their face is lined with age. They discard their spouse in search of beauty and excitement. If only they would peel back the layers, the wrapping, and discover the depth in that aged body—the person who stood with them through the agonizing, challenging, and joyful years of life. But they look for beauty elsewhere and often find that beneath the wrapping is something significantly inferior in worth to what they had before.

Every day is a surprise for the two of us—serendipity. I live with constant gratitude that God spared Jay and Paul. Paul lives with a deep sense of joy that he is alive and can see his children and grandchildren grow into flourishing human beings. Paul and Jay both bear scars, but they are beautiful to me.

I urge you not to take the people in your life for granted. Appreciate them with all their flaws and their brokenness. Sometimes there is a depth of beauty beneath that brokenness that is as pure as a crystal stream and runs very deep. Search for it until you find it. Stop to smell the roses and splash in the rain and the mud. Take time to smile at the person in his wheelchair and greet the old worn face with a lovely soul.

Beauty is everywhere if you look for it. God made a stunning world, but the most magnificent of all the things God ever made was you. He made you in His image, and that means you are unique. Appreciate all of God's vast and amazing creation.

I see the immense beauty in my family; with all their scars and imperfections they are simply lovely. And every day—snow, rain or sunshine—I rise and say, "Another beautiful day. Thank you, Jesus!"

 *Chapter 14*

A Reluctant Student Receives Affirmation in the Halls of Academia

*A man of great memory without learning hath
a rock and a spindle and no staff to spin.*

GEORGE HERBERT

OUR DAUGHTER HAS AN EXCEPTIONAL memory. She also has another extraordinary ability, and that is to conceal secrets. She is like a pirate hoarding treasure. Once a secret is safely ensconced with her, nothing and no one will ever extract the information from its safekeeping.

But when she does want to impart something, it seems all she needs to do is access a file in her brain and draw the information out. She obviously has her filing system neatly organized, because you can ask her the phone number of one of our parishioners from fourteen years ago and she will rattle it off without hesitation.

I am quick to acknowledge that she has her dad's genes, and I am thankful for that.

I don't give secrets away either, but that is probably because they get lost. Most information seems to filter through my mind, and then somewhere en route to my memory box it goes astray and is dumped into my forgotten bin, or is vaporized, never to be retrieved again.

So when I was presented the opportunity to do further studies, I was quite adamant that I should not. I had my master's degree and I felt that doing a PhD in my forties was somewhat risky. My memory was not as sharp as it had once been, and I certainly did not think that I had the time to begin the rigorous work demanded of a doctoral program.

My life was also extremely busy at that time. I was lecturing and leading the BA leadership program at Mattersey, and I was out most weekends preaching or promoting the college with Paul. Did I want to take on another load? Absolutely not! However, the more I pondered the opportunity, the more convinced I became that the Lord wanted me to pursue my PhD. Paul and I had done a lot of traveling and preaching in the UK. I had become increasingly perplexed at the state of the churches in the Assemblies of God in Great Britain, the denomination to which we related.

In the first six weeks of us arriving in the UK, we traveled and ministered in a number of different churches. In every church we spoke at in those first few months, Paul and I were the youngest people in the church. I found this alarming and disconcerting.

It was becoming more and more apparent to me that Europe was secularized and that the UK was seeing rampant decline in the attendance of young people in their churches. Of course, this was not the case with every church; like most places around the world, there were churches that were doing well. But generally, from my perspective, the situation was bleak. Where we see hundreds of mega churches in the United States, the UK has only a small handful.

As I prayed, I felt my heart becoming burdened for the country in which I was serving, and a longing was birthed in my heart to help our denomination. Without over-spiritualizing my academic journey, I can say with certainty that the reason I embarked on this journey was because I loved Jesus and His church.

My heart ached for the leaders of our denomination, and I wanted to add to my learning, so that in some small way I could help others in their pilgrimage.

Moving around the nation, I encountered some leaders who were disillusioned. The shifts in culture were challenging for them, and straddling the modern and postmodern paradigms was particularly disconcerting for some. In fact, I recall an older leader saying, "I don't understand young people today. I have no idea how they tick and what goes on in their heads. I am going to resign and leave it all up to them." That particular statement hammered into my brain with a forceful blow, perplexing me and keeping me awake at night.

Most often my thoughts would be troubled in the early hours of the morning. In the mauve-tinged moments of daybreak, as night slipped away, the faces of leaders and the state of the church would come before my mind.

One thing I was convinced of was that we could not afford to lose the wealth of experience that older leaders had to offer. Yes, we needed younger leaders desperately; their creativity, flexibility, and flair were all necessary characteristics for the future well-being of the church. But we could never underestimate the value and wisdom of older men and women. I did not want to see either group lost to the church in the twenty-first century.

We had lived in Australia and encountered postmodern philosophy in its most aggressive form. I recall when we moved there, one of the men unpacking our boxes quizzically remarked, "You have a lot of books?" Paul told him that we were both avid readers and many of the books were related to the work we did. He inquired what line of work we were in. Paul responded enthusiastically, "I am a pastor."

The man looked at Paul in surprise and said, "Really! What does a pastor do?"

Paul tried to meet the man on his own terms. "Well, I am like a priest."

By now the man unpacking our boxes had stopped and was looking at Paul with big, questioning eyes. He asked, "Well, what does a priest do?"

Paul was beginning to enjoy the conversation and was anticipating where it was going. "I am responsible for the people in my parish church.

They come to church every Sunday, and I teach them and encourage them to grow in faith and their love for God."

The man was flabbergasted and inquired, "Are you telling me that those buildings with stained-glass windows are not museums, but places where people go and listen to teaching?"

We realized that this man was so secular that he had not encountered a single Christian until this point. That was our baptism into a secularized society.

England was just as secular, if not more. I remember how stunned I was to discover how many young people who called themselves Christ followers had mixed morals and a limited understanding of a Christian worldview. They delighted in Jesus, but wanted little to do with the demands of the Christian life. They seemed capable of living comfortably with conflicting beliefs and saw no problem with some of the morally ambiguous positions in society, which often led to living paradoxical lives. Some of them had a strong commitment to justice and poverty while believing it was perfectly acceptable to have sex before marriage.

Into that climate we found ourselves ministering to a new generation of people in a strange and different world.

With all the cultural and authority shifts taking place in Western society and the many moral ambiguities we were encountering, I felt that I was discovering a project that could captivate my attention for a PhD. And so it was that my academic journey began once again.

I was reluctant, but I knew beyond a shadow of doubt that God wanted me to walk this pathway.

Memories of my school years came flashing back. Is it not strange how moments that have been hidden in the deep recesses of your mind can surface with such ferocity? I hated school. All those horrid remembrances came creeping back through the crevices of my mind, their sinister echoes seemingly intent on hammering out any hope of success in my academic career.

I had done my schooling in South Africa in the 1960s. For the slightest infraction you were given the strap, or what we called "cuts."

If you spelled a word incorrectly or your writing was untidy, you would put out your hand at the teacher's request. She or he would hold a ruler over your heads and then come down with incredible force, leaving red welts on your skin.

If your spelling offense or writing was really terrible, the lashing could be repeated up to five times. Whispering to a friend while standing in line was strictly forbidden, and if you were caught, the teacher would sneak up on you and the ruler would come down behind your knees in a severe blow, leaving red marks as a telltale sign of your bad conduct.

As I write, I can still feel the agony of those awful lashings. I always thought it was unfair to be lashed for the minor misdemeanor of not knowing how to spell a word or add up sums correctly. I was a compliant child, always wanting to please my teacher, but even I could not avoid some of those dreadful whippings.

Of course, it was not helpful that in the early stages of pursuing my PhD I had some rather harsh supervision. All my insecurities seemed to return with a vengeance, and there were times I felt as if I could simply give it all up. But I persisted. I recall there were days where I put my head down on my desk and cried out to the Lord, "I am not capable of doing this. I need your help. Please clear my mind and enable me to understand and process the information I am gleaning."

After almost three years of working on my PhD, with my confidence at a very low ebb, a mentor and friend, Dr. William Kay, asked me if I would like to transfer the supervision of my PhD to him. I wanted to kiss him, but I knew that would be inappropriate, so I simply said, "That would be marvelous, and can we start immediately?" He agreed and we promptly began working.

I felt that God was intervening once again on my behalf. He had seen my struggles and how I had persisted despite some of the discouraging moments in the journey, and now He was sending help my way.

In just over another year I was able to complete my entire PhD under Dr. Kay's supervision. His expertise and vast knowledge helped me immensely. But he also respected me and would listen to my findings and show interest in my data collection and analysis. My confidence slowly built and I began to write with renewed passion and self-assurance.

As the time for my *viva voce* ("living voice," which is a live exam) approached, I began to feel increasingly apprehensive. Part of the process of completing a PhD in the UK requires you to have a *viva voce* exam to make a defense for the research and work you have completed.

You go before a panel of academics—usually an internal examiner from the university that you have undertaken your PhD with, an external examiner who is considered an expert in the field of your research, and then a chair who directs the process and ensures order and equity throughout the exam.

For me personally, this was the most challenging aspect of my PhD. When people showed surprise at my apprehension and said in amazement, "You are a public speaker. You preach to large crowds. Why would you be apprehensive about defending your work in front of a small group of people?" I would always reply emphatically, "I am defending the greatest piece of work in my entire life. Well ... why wouldn't I be nervous?" If I failed, then four years of agonizing effort would be to no avail.

There were a number of complicating circumstances surrounding the final stages of my PhD. The details are unimportant, but they seemed insurmountable to me. However, what it meant for me was that I only knew who my examiners were a few months before my *viva*. This was disconcerting to me, because it meant that I could not get acquainted with their work and prepare myself from that perspective.

In the hours between night and day, I would lie in bed and feel anxiety creep over me and enshroud me like a heavy cloud. Paul was getting frustrated with my lack of confidence and my sheer anxiety about defending my work. He was aware of the hours I had invested into this project, and he had walked with me every painful step of the journey.

One day, I sat down and shared where my deep insecurity had its roots. In the early phases of my work my supervisor (not the gracious Dr. Kay) had written more than once that my writing style was pedestrian, which simply put means dull and lacking vitality. On other occasions he had made similar remarks, which slowly whittled away at my confidence. His words played over and over in my mind like a broken record.

My *viva voce* was set for early May. Unfortunately, Paul was away at the time. Our faithful personal assistant, Ruth Brightwell, agreed to drive me to Wales to go before the panel. She was gracious and knew that I would want to relax on the journey up and not have to bother with fighting traffic along the way.

We left the day before my appearance. Paul had booked us into a quaint little bed-and-breakfast just a mile from the university. The night before my exam, I probably reached the lowest point of my entire journey. I sat in my little room and thought, *Yes, this work is not good. I have not written well at all.* The words of my previous supervisor pounded in my head: *"Your style of writing is dull . . . boring!"*

I closed the hard copy of my work and said to myself, "I am never going to lecture again. I am not cut out for this. This PhD is going to be thrown in the trash as soon as this whole process is over." I switched off the light, prayed earnestly, and slept fitfully through the night.

I am certain that some of our discouragement is sinister and has its origins in dark places. In the week leading up to my *viva*, five different people shared their experiences of their oral exams with me. Every single one of them had a referral (this occurs when the examiners require that further work be done on the dissertation) of six months or longer. Not one of the people I spoke to had experienced success.

I had also prayed earnestly that my internal examiner would not be a philosopher. Not only did I discover that she was indeed a philosopher, but she was also an expert on the German philosopher Nietzsche. Can you wonder at my anxiety the evening before my panel appearance?

I awoke the next morning and was thankful that it was a bright day and the rain had managed to hold off for once. I went to breakfast and determined to eat everything on the menu.

After breakfast I went for a long walk and prayed earnestly for success. I tried to push the negative thoughts out of my brain, but they would occasionally rear their ugly head through the clouds of my mind. However,

I kept praying and seeking God's help and guidance. I knew that I had prepared myself adequately. I had thought through every possible question I could be asked. I'd prepared myself for complex questions that demanded my attention and rapid thinking. I had memorized my opening remarks and had thought through carefully what I would say to an examiner who assessed the rigor of my work.

Ruth and I left the bed-and-breakfast with ample time to find parking and for me to find the room in which the examination was taking place. We got to the university and there was not a spare parking place to be found within ten minutes of the campus. As anxiety crept over me, a young Chinese student pulled out of his parking spot and ushered us into the opening. I said a hasty, "Thank you, Lord!" I was certain that He had planned that little serendipitous start for me.

Ruth prayed with me, and then we decided that I would give her a call once my exam was over.

I walked apprehensively to the building that housed my exam room. I went slowly up the stairs, my heart beating in my chest. I strode down the long, sterile corridor of the grand stone building and was met by the delightful lady who had organized the details of this day. She rushed out to greet me, her friendliness heartening as she directed me to the exam room.

I walked past the room and I saw my two examiners through the glass panel; they were in the throes of a serious discussion. My heart pounded violently. I went and stood as far away from the room as I could. I did not want to hear them discussing my dismal work.

As I stood there, my hands trembling and my mouth beginning to get that metallic taste of fear, leaving my tongue clinging to my palate like sandpaper, the chairman of the exam committee walked purposefully toward me. He saw me, and a smile spread across his face as he came over and embraced me. I have to say I felt quite overwhelmed.

In a moment of utter vulnerability I said, "Wow, I am nervous!" He looked at me, and with a voice booming with confidence, he said, "You will do just fine, my dear."

At this juncture I was beginning to think that the Lord had organized all these little greetings to cheer me up before facing my adversaries in that dismal exam room. I was slowly starting to feel a little less anxious and believing that God had heard the desperate cry of my heart.

After standing outside the room for a number of minutes, I was formally called to enter the examination room and begin the most dreaded part of my entire academic journey. The chairman greeted everyone and introduced me to my examiners. He then invited me to share briefly with the panel what my PhD was about.

I had practiced this bit over and over, but I found myself sharing with passion the work that God had led me to do and the results of my empirical research. As I finished he looked at me and complimented me on a succinct and lively introduction to my work. I was thinking, *Wow, everyone told me that the examiners on the panel were your adversaries—unfriendly, out to trip you up. God, you must be encouraging me here.*

I was still thinking these thoughts when my external examiner looked at me and said, "You have written a very long piece of work."

I had anticipated that this could be a problem. Dr. Kay had warned me that my PhD was longer than most and that it could be a potential problem. "However," the examiner continued, "I found your work very interesting." And then he asked me the first question.

By this time, I was fully convinced that God was right there in that room with me. He was encouraging me through the words of the panel.

All eyes moved to my internal examiner, the Nietzsche philosopher. I met her gaze as she looked at me and said, "I have to agree with our external examiner that your work was lengthy." I was slightly anxious at this point. Your internal examiner is supposed to be the friendly person in the room, and if she couldn't see the value of my work, I was in serious trouble. She continued, "But I read every single word of your work. You have a very engaging style of writing, and it kept my attention through all the pages."

Remember, before going to my *viva*, the words, *Your writing style is dull and boring . . . It is not of an academic standard,* had tumbled over and over in my mind. Now I sat before these notable academics, and they were commending me. At that moment I knew beyond any doubt that God was affirming my work and me.

The examination was rigorous to the end. I sat in that room and answered questions for over an hour. I was drilled about my empirical research and the size of my sample group. But through the entire process I held my ground and argued my points with confidence and clarity. Finally, the chairman of the panel congratulated me on my exam and asked me to exit the room while the examiners discussed my performance.

I left the room and looked at my watch. Every person who had told me about their experience had advised me to check my watch, because they said I could sit and wait for an hour or more while the examiners discussed whether my work was of a satisfactory standard. They assured me that the hour could feel a lot longer while the panel deliberated.

After six minutes I was called back into the room. The thought went swirling through my mind, "*This is either good news, or it is decisively bad news.*"

I walked into the room somewhat apprehensively. My external examiner put out his hand and shook mine, saying cheerfully, "Congratulations, Dr. Alexander!"

It was the sweetest sound my ears had heard, the sound of reward for years of hard work. Those were three words that I never thought I would hear.

I bade everyone on the panel farewell and I literally floated down two flights of stairs. I do not know if I passed anyone along the way; I was literally on a cloud wafting through space and time with a smile on my face that would not go away.

I got down to the parking lot and phoned Ruth. I knew it would take her a full ten minutes to get to me, so I wanted to be sure to call her immediately. I did not tell her how I had done because I wanted Paul to be the first person to hear the news. Of course, this left her feeling anxious as she hurried to meet me.

I pressed Paul's number and waited for his familiar, happy voice to answer. He was traveling on a train from London and I had promised I would phone him directly after my *viva voce*. He read the caller ID and answered the phone with unusual anxiety. "Hello! Cam?"

When I heard Paul's voice, the fountains of the deep broke and I began weeping uncontrollably. Years of hard work, moments of stress and anxiety, failed confidence and lack of sleep, all caught up in that moment of hearing his voice, and I sobbed uncontrollably while I tried desperately to get some words out my mouth. Of course, Paul instantly suspected the worst—until he heard me say, "I am a doctor of philosophy." And then I just heard his voice crack and he couldn't speak for a number of minutes.

We sat on the phone and we both cried. I was the first person in my family line to ever achieve this status. It is a sweet and lasting memory that has lingered with me through all these years and, I am certain, will not diminish with time. More than anything else, I know that Jesus journeyed each step of the way with me. And He so evidently revealed that to me through the process of my oral exam.

This simple South African girl, from an ordinary family in an insignificant town, had taken a journey way outside of her comfort zone and had achieved what she thought she never could.

Ruth arrived to collect me. She got out the car and rushed up to me with anxiety etched into every part of her face. With red, swollen eyes I told her the good news, and we hugged in one jubilant and joyful moment.

My mom and dad, my two sisters, my brother, and our children all came to my graduation. It was a very moving occasion and a milestone in my journey as a Christian leader.

Reflection

I have always been thankful for the privilege I have had of learning and achieving a PhD. It was not something I ever wanted to do, but Jesus clearly led me and helped me through the entire process. Every single thing I do has had one simple goal: to extend God's kingdom on earth. There is nothing I have done in my life without that as my primary motivation.

I am not a natural academic, but I am an ardent believer in doing things with excellence. I also happen to believe that Christian leaders should give themselves to lifelong learning. It was said of David in Psalm 78:72, "And David shepherded them with integrity of heart; / with skillful hands he led them." I am certain David spent hours harnessing his skills as a young shepherd boy. He developed his ability with a sling while he was out in the desert, tending sheep. He played his harp honing his musical abilities in the lonely hours of the night. He worked constantly at acquiring and sharpening skills. It is incumbent upon leaders to harness their abilities and equip themselves to be useful in their Master's hands.

I do believe that if we want to stay engaged and active, we should commit ourselves to learning. I trust that if you are in the process of developing some skill and you feel discouraged, my story will encourage you to go all the way. I know that my journey filled me with wild hope and the belief that nothing is impossible if we try and we believe.

 *Chapter 15*

Joy in Ellendale, North Dakota

When large numbers of people share their joy in common, the happiness of each is greater because each adds fuel to the other's flame.

ST. AUGUSTINE

CHARCOAL CLOUDS GATHERED ON THE horizon. The sky looked angry and the sound of thunder came rumbling through the trees that stood around our house. I could smell the rain in the air as lightning streaked across the blackened skies. The ominous weather seemed a mirror image of what was happening in our lives.

As I peered through the window of my little English house, sheets of rain began to pour down, and the earth seemed to drink with relish. I was amazed as I watched the ground absorb each drop of liquid. I pondered at how the earth could possibly be thirsty because these English skies were relentless in showering down profuse amounts of water onto this little island. I gazed in amazement at the seemingly thirsty earth gulping each droplet. This was a greedy land that never appeared satisfied.

We were in the throes of packing up our home to leave Mattersey Hall College and Graduate School and return to the US. We had been serving at Mattersey for seven years and living in the president's house on the campus.

Moving my home is one of the things I enjoy least, and sorting through what we should take and what we should leave behind seemed an insurmountable task. Constant moving had taught me to become quite ruthless and emotionally detached from material items, which meant that I often parted with dearly loved objects in a moment of weakness, only to regret it at some later stage. However, there is nothing quite like moving to get rid of stuff and clear out some of those items that haven't been used in a long time.

We had known for about six months that we would be leaving. Our departure was tinged with some unnecessary sadness, but I had a deep internal peace that God was watching over us. And I was right.

We had not wanted to destabilize the Mattersey community in any way. Nor did we want enrollment to suffer. So we had carefully thought through when we would announce our departure to the community we had loved and served for so many years.

We were sitting in a chapel service one day, at a time when none of our community knew we were leaving. A young African woman came up to me filled with emotion and said, "You are going to birth something new in God." I was slightly taken aback, because I knew that no one could possibly be aware that we were leaving.

The following week during chapel service, another young woman came up to me and with passion dripping from her lips exclaimed, "You are pregnant with a vision that God will shortly bring to pass."

I knew that God was with us and that our lives and our future were secure in His hands, but the word from these two young women was encouraging to me.

Sometimes, when our lives take twists and turns that we never anticipated, we wonder where God is in our circumstances. But I have learned that if you are God's child and your life is committed to His cause, His plan will always prevail. Even when the situation is bleak and you cannot imagine how God could possibly be involved in your plight, He is there.

I think of Joseph in Genesis 37–50—his narrative is an encouraging one because through each season of his life, it is evident that God was weaving His plan for Joseph's life and for the lives of the Israelites. Joseph was treated harshly and unfairly, but you get the sense from the biblical text that he knew God had a destiny for his life and nothing could thwart that. Men could try their best, or their worst, but ultimately Joseph believed that God would have His way.

When people mistreat you and there is grave injustice, God can and always does turn those situations for good. The only responsibility we have is to ensure our hearts never become bitter or angry. Through all the challenging seasons of life and ministry, Paul and I have always endeavored to keep our hearts free of negativity.

Our last few weeks were busy weeks with our daily schedules of lecturing and leading as well as packing up and preparing to leave. Three of our friends and mentors walked a close journey with us through this time, and we were able to share our hearts, our disappointments, and our dreams with them.

I will always think of our pastor, Ken Williamson, and our friends Dave Shearman, and Phil Jones as three amazing individuals who walked relentlessly beside us, embracing us and loving us through our final months in the UK. How can we ever say thank you enough?

On Friday morning, October 14, 2011, I had a dream. I do realize that there is nothing unusual about dreaming, but generally I have absurd dreams. I dream most nights and it seems from the images that are conjured in my mind during my unconscious hours that my brain fires at an alarmingly rapid rate, which finds me accomplishing feats that in my wakened state are nigh impossible.

When I woke up in the early hours of Friday morning with a clear, intelligent, and carefully constructed dream, I knew it had come from God.

It was five a.m. when I sat straight up from the impact of my vision. I usually wake up feeling sluggish and disoriented until I've had my morning cup of tea. Most mornings I have to ask Paul what day it is, and sometimes I even ask him where we are. However, on this particular morning I was alert and my mind was crystal clear. I felt the need to articulate the lucid contents of the images I had just seen. With real urgency in my voice I said, "Paul, wake up. I have had a dream."

To my dismay, he shuffled, then he grunted, then he graciously patted my head and replied, "Mmm, go back to sleep, darling."

Let me assure you that there was no possibility of me going back to sleep after my dream.

My dream had come in two distinct parts. The first scene was what we were leaving. The details are unimportant to this story, but the curtain closed on that portion of the dream and it was as if God was showing me that particular phase of our lives was over. I felt God was saying, "It is time to move to the next chapter of your lives."

The curtain opened with scene two.

Paul and I were both sitting in a car. It was stationary, which made perfect sense, because we had decided to take a six-month sabbatical and so we would be sitting still for a period of time. Well, let me rephrase that! We had no day-to-day responsibilities of any sort. However, we did have a number of preaching engagements in the US and other parts of the world.

For us, the lack of responsibility and the freedom from the daily challenges of leadership was a blessed period of relief. It would be a rejuvenating and refreshing time for both of us. And it would ignite us and reinvigorate us for what God had for us in our future, which at that point we were oblivious to.

Back to the dream.

We were both sitting in this car, and Paul had his hands on the steering wheel in readiness for our next journey. As we sat waiting, I suddenly became aware of something on the backseat of our car. I turned around and saw a baby lying there. I looked at the lifeless form of this baby and began to weep. Turning toward Paul, my voice filled with emotion, I cried, "The baby is dead. The baby is dead." I was weeping inconsolably. Paul put his head on the steering wheel and we both wept together.

For some reason I had a compulsion to turn around and touch the cold, listless form of the baby. I extended my hand towards the baby and as I touched the seemingly lifeless body, it stirred. I was overjoyed. I looked at Paul and exclaimed, "The baby is alive. It's alive."

We both started to laugh as I picked up the baby and began to nurture it. As I cared for the little one in my arms, I woke up from my dream.

When we were eating breakfast that morning I tried to bring the conversation around to my dream. I knew I was fighting a losing battle because Paul simply said that he had a busy day ahead of him and he needed to get to the office. I had a feeling he knew my dream had special significance, and perhaps he wasn't ready or willing to listen to it.

The dream remained in my consciousness throughout the day, and the more I reflected on its contents, the more I realized that indeed there was special significance to it.

We came home after we had finished our lunch in the college cafeteria. We had our daily ritual of going back to our home after lunch and making a cup of tea. I am a firm believer that tea is the cure to many of life's ailments. So whenever we are challenged or need to reflect on a situation, the kettle goes on and the teapot comes out.

I also believe in brewing a *good* cup of tea, and that means you need good-quality tealeaves. There is a necessary step-by-step procedure for making a good pot of tea. First, boil the water; that is the most important step. Second, pour some of the boiling water into the teapot to warm it up. When the pot is nice and hot, pour the water out and add the tea leaves, and then fill the pot with boiling water. Cover with a tea cozy and let it sit for five minutes. Once the tea leaves have slowly settled at the bottom of the teapot, pour some milk into a porcelain china cup and then fill it to the brim with the amber liquid. Finally, lift the cup to your lips and slowly sip the heavenly nectar. You will feel life flowing back into your veins as you slowly drain every last drop of the delicious brew. I recommend it!

As I sat in my lounge, overlooking the fishpond and the weeping willow tree in my backyard, I put my head back and prayed, "God, if this dream is from you, I need to understand what it means." I had not even finished my sentence when the meaning came to me. God said to me, *"That is your next assignment."*

Initially Paul and I were not sure what "the dead baby" represented. We wondered if we would be working with orphans in Africa or something else. However, I was not concerned about our future because I knew that God had a pretty clear picture of where He would be sending us. After all,

I had been quite specific in describing all the details of my desired place of service to the Lord.

I had told God that I had suffered dismal weather for long enough and I knew that He understood perfectly well that I wanted to escape the grey, cold weather that I had been unduly subjected to for the past seven years. I even specified the trees and the fruit that would grow in the place He was sending us to.

I told the Lord I wanted white sandy beaches with palm trees, mangoes, pineapples, coconuts and perpetual sunshine. I didn't actually specify Hawaii, but I knew God was clever enough to know this important detail. However, I wanted to leave my options open with the Almighty, and since I knew Hawaii might be a long shot, I decided Florida or California would be a great second best.

So there! All done! Prayer request had gone heavenward . . . everything would be arranged. God knew exactly where I wanted to go and He would be certain to organize the details in order to accomplish the desires of my heart.

You can only imagine my shock when Paul came to me one day and said, "There is a small school in Ellendale, North Dakota . . . They are looking for a president . . . They want us to go and do a spiritual emphasis week." I knew immediately that this could not possibly be in God's plan for our lives. After all, no one who wants to do something significant for God goes to North Dakota.

I looked at a map of Ellendale and was convinced beyond a shadow of a doubt that this was definitely not in the purpose of God. The town had fifteen hundred people in it. Ridiculous! Everyone knows you do not go from Europe to Ellendale to serve God. We wanted to make an impact for God's kingdom and I was persuaded that Ellendale was not the place to do so.

So I looked at Paul with determined resolve and said, "Why waste our time? God would never want us to go to such an insignificant little place."

I had not been aware that Trinity Bible College even existed before that particular moment. However, it has always amazed me the ways in which God weaves His plan together. Over thirty years before this time, Roland Dudley had made a brief stopover at our college in South Africa, and it was there we first became acquainted with him. Our paths would cross over the years until he came back into our lives while we were serving at Mattersey.

Roland and his lovely wife, Judy, were leading Continental Theological Seminary in Brussels at the same time we were leading Mattersey. He served as president there for thirteen years.

Now all these years later, Roland and Judy were serving as missionaries in residence at Trinity Bible College. It was Roland who strategized to get us to Trinity to do a spiritual emphasis week.

We were ministering in the Chicago area and so Paul suggested we push through to Ellendale and do the spiritual emphasis week for the college. Reluctantly I complied—and I cannot stress the word *reluctantly* enough! I wanted Paul to understand that there was absolutely no possibility of us ever going to North Dakota on a permanent basis. After all, God knew I needed sunshine, blue skies, and white beaches.

We arrived on the campus of Trinity Bible College on January 19, 2012. It was a bitterly cold day. I remember that it was 19 degrees below freezing. I was ill equipped for the brutal weather, and I felt the biting-cold wind hitting me with a velocity that made me breathless and chilled me to the core.

This was the first sight that we saw as we drove up Main Street towards Trinity Bible College. Our hearts were strangely warmed as we saw this majestic building.

I walked outside all prim and proper in my North Carolina winter coat, which was not even warm enough for a Dakotan spring. I had fashionable shoes, which allowed the cold to seep into all the openings, rendering my feet numb and almost useless.

Sam Johnson showed us around the campus, and I remember thinking how beautiful it was. The only problem was that I was so icy cold my lips were tinged blue, and my teeth ached to such an extent that I couldn't speak to let him know how lovely everything was.

As we walked around the college, my feet got colder and colder, and at one point I was convinced they would fall off the end of my legs. This was all confirming my initial thoughts that God could never possibly want to use us in this barren cold land. I have never in my life experienced such bitter cold.

By the time we walked back to where we'd started the tour, all my pride had vanished; I took the pretty scarf that was simply adorning my neck with charm and I wrapped it around my face and my mouth. I put the hood of my coat over my head, and all anyone could see was my pair of green eyes. I looked like an Egyptian mummy and I didn't care! That is what happens to you when you go to North Dakota.

After our tour, we went into the magnificent four-hundred-seat chapel to preach. We sat on the platform with some of the faculty members, which gave us a panoramic view of everyone in the chapel. People looked austere and somber.

I remember gazing out over the student body and feeling immense sadness. I turned to Paul and said, "This place is dead, and these students are lifeless." I know it sounds harsh, and it could be perceived as criticism, but it was not said with any malice or guile. There was a genuine ache in my heart. I had this sense that the place was dying.

Paul got up to preach and as he did I felt the atmosphere changing. By the time he concluded, I was amazed at the enthusiastic response of the student body. I looked at Paul and said, "Maybe there is still life in this place after all." I was not thinking of my dream at this point.

We stayed on the campus for a couple of days. The longer I was there, the more my heart warmed to Trinity. I really could not understand it, because from a human perspective the place had no appeal for me. Ellendale, North Dakota, was not on my bucket list. Hawaii was!

On the second day, some of the board members asked to meet with Paul and me. We sat in a little conference room and the atmosphere was slightly awkward. The members of the board were probably unsure of how to start a conversation, and we were definitely not certain that we even wanted to have this meeting. We were feeling apprehensive and uncertain. We chatted about everything under the sun except the issue at hand.

Eventually the conversation came around to Trinity. We spoke for some time about the college, and then one of the board members looked at us and said, "I am going to be honest with you. About a year ago we wondered if Trinity could survive. We asked ourselves, "Is the baby dead?"

I thought, "Whoa, wait a second. This is scary. I have heard those words before, and they were in a dream!"

He continued. "But we felt that if someone would pick it up and nurture it [now he was using the same words I had used to articulate my dream], it could come back to life. [He used my words again.]"

Let me add, that this particular board member does not generally articulate himself in this manner, but God was using him to speak directly to us.

I had only shared my dream with Paul and three close friends who all lived in the UK. There is no way this board member could possibly have known any of the details of my dream—and yet in a few brief seconds he had described my dream in vivid detail. I was overwhelmed. In that moment my heart bowed in submission to Jesus. I knew that Trinity was the "dead baby" and I understood that God wanted us to pick up this vision and nurture it back to full health.

I realized that God had a plan for Trinity and that He wanted Paul and me to be a part of that plan. Yes, I wanted white sandy beaches and sunshine, but God knew what my heart really needed, and that was a place called Trinity Bible College in Ellendale, North Dakota.

And so, in this season of our lives, Paul and I are leading Trinity

Bible College in the prairies. I sometimes remind myself that a place like Nazareth was considered small and insignificant. It was a tiny agricultural village with no trade routes and no economic importance, and the population was probably around a mere five hundred people. Yet it was this inconsequential little place that nurtured Jesus, preparing him for his future life and ministry.

We moved to Ellendale, North Dakota, on July 1, 2012. It is a significant date for us, although it certainly was not planned that way. It was exactly nine months after the two ladies had told me that I was pregnant with a new vision. It was also the date of our son's accident, when he was found lifeless and not breathing at the scene of the accident. As God gave us our "dead" son back, so we believed that God was giving the "dead baby" Trinity back to North Dakota.

The first few weeks at Trinity were extremely challenging and trying ones for us. I am certain if we had not had clear direction from God, we would have been tempted to abandon the project. There was a lot of unhappiness among the faculty, students were disgruntled, and the financial situation of the college was dismal. In God's perfect timing he sent Winston Titus to serve as vice president of administration. Under his skilled and watchful eye the college has slowly come through to financial health.

We soon discovered that the student body was significantly less than we thought and that the college had been placed on academic probation. There were other findings that sent us reeling in different directions, but throughout that whole time we felt sustained by the God who had brought us to our Nazareth. None of these facts are a reflection on any particular person. I am simply relaying facts, and it would be disingenuous of me to say otherwise. We do understand that decline is not a sudden event; it is slow and steady and many factors play into it.

We are thankful that the board and Sam Johnson's tenacity and love for the college ensured that the doors did not close and the baby did not die. There have also been many generous friends of the college whose names I cannot mention but whose love and generosity kept Trinity's doors open. To all of them we owe a profound debt of gratitude. To our beloved friends Sam and Joyce Johnson: Trinity is eternally indebted to you. And to the board: thank you for keeping the baby alive.

Since arriving two years ago, we have seen God do many wonderful things on our campus. In my view, of all the things He has done, the greatest has been in the spiritual life of the people. This community has been transformed into one of the happiest places on the planet.

Our chapel services are vibrant, and our students and faculty are passionate in their love and devotion to God and to this community. I love Trinity more than my words can express, and I am grateful to God for bringing Paul and me here.

We have already started refurbishing one of our old buildings—the hundred-year-old Davidson Hall. A generous donor gave a million dollars, ensuring that we have not had to incur a penny's debt. We also had an old, run-down administrative building that caused Paul bouts of anxiety. Truth be told, the building embarrassed him because it was in such shocking condition.

Every morning, as he walked to his office, he had to stare at the unsightly structure for over one hundred and thirty paces. He learned to hate it! He would walk past and feel stressed. He decided to start praying about the building so that his blood pressure wouldn't continue to rise every morning as he faced the obnoxious sight. As he prayed, he felt God wanted him to replace the building with a prayer chapel—a reflective space where our students could go and meditate in quiet solitude.

The plans kept growing as different people made suggestions, and eventually the new plan was a chapel, with three classrooms and adjoining corridors that connected the entire campus—meaning people never have to walk outside in the winter months. We were unsure where the money would come from, but Paul had faith to believe that God would provide.

It was during that time that Paul felt a strong compulsion to go and visit a couple whom we had befriended over the previous two years and ask them to be anchor donors for the project. He was naturally apprehensive, but his first meeting was positive, and they decided to visit the college. We had a feeling that they might be prepared to give us much as half a million dollars to the first part of the project.

We were alarmed when we heard our friends were visiting the campus while we were away ministering in the UK. However, our competent leaders on campus were able to clearly articulate Paul's vision. At the end of their visit they informed the small group they had met with that they were not giving a half a million dollars, but instead were going to give the full two million dollars for the entire project. We got an e-mail early the next morning that gave us the news. As we read the words, we wept in amazement and gratitude.

God has brought life and health back to the baby.

There have been other miracles along the way. Generous donors have given money to restore the old president's house—a beautiful hundred-year-old Victorian home. We are staggered at all that God has done in the past two years. And the best is yet to come. This is just the beginning. We are excited to see what God is going to do in the future, and we anticipate Trinity growing in many different dimensions. I suppose that story will have to be told in another volume.

And so this little South African girl from an ordinary family finds herself living on the plains of North Dakota with the man God promised her when she was sixteen years old. We never imagined that we could feel so fulfilled and happy.

We wake up every day with anticipation in our hearts and wonder what exciting thing God is going to do through us this day. Yes, we have experienced some of the darkest nights, we have known depths of pain we did not think possible to bear. Yet through every moment God has been there.

We have no apprehension in our hearts for the future because we know God is already there. We are certain He is in control of the events of our lives and we know that He has a plan for Trinity.

We are grateful that our destiny collided with Trinity Bible College.

Here we are able to watch godly men and women prepare for servant ministry in a world that desperately needs the touch of the Nazarene. As they study in secluded Ellendale, God is preparing an army of meek and gentle yet strong men and women who have a passion to see broken lives mended and dysfunctional families restored to health and wholeness.

God didn't give me white sandy beaches or palm trees. He didn't give me sunny blue skies, mangoes, or coconuts. Instead He gave me the quiet stillness of the plains—beautiful, serene Ellendale, North Dakota. And for that I am thankful.

The beautiful campus of Trinity Bible College and Graduate School in Ellendale, North Dakota. Since 2012 millions of dollars have been spent on its continued development.

Reflection

I refer again to Psalm 139 as it is one of my favorite psalms. It says in verse 16, " Your eyes saw my unformed body; / all the days ordained for me were written in your book before one of them came to be." This verse reminds me that nothing ever happens by chance. God is in absolute control of the world and of our lives. I am still simple enough to believe He is involved in every aspect of our lives, and that if we commit our way to Him, then He will direct our paths. I encourage you to stop and reflect on God's goodness in your life and remind yourself that your life is in His safe hands.

I trust that as you have read my journey you have been inspired with the same wild hope that has infused Paul's veins and mine. My earnest prayer is that your life will be enriched and you will discover God in all His majesty and beauty. I can recommend my Jesus. He is beautiful beyond description. I do know that if I had to do it all over again I would not change anything.

Author's Note

I grow very fond of this place, and it certainly
has a desolate, grim beauty of its own,
that has a curious fascination for me.

THEODORE ROOSEVELT

I WOKE AT DAWN THIS morning to watch the sunrise in Ellendale. I love the African skies, but there is a mystique and a stillness in the plains that is captivating. How can I do justice in trying to describe a Dakotan sunrise? The sky is like an ocean of peach-colored waves that filter through smoky-grey clouds tinged with lavender. I stop and pause, to listen, and to gaze. Birds fly in the amber glow, singing their cheerful song. The night is over and the morning has come—wild hope for a new day.

The sad moments of yesterday seem to dissipate as the soft, gentle rays of the morning sun wash over me. The promise of a new day ignites a passion in me and dispels any misgivings for the hours ahead. I glance out over the fields; the wheat is bathed in an apricot glow and leaves on the trees dance in the gentle breeze, absorbing the peachy light emanating from the sky. The grass shivers in the breeze. This is home.

Life is simple here—there is no pretending. I have lived on four continents, in big cities, small towns, and quaint villages. However, no place has touched me as deeply as North Dakota. I am not even certain that I can articulate with any clarity why it moves me. Perhaps it is because of the simplicity of life here. I don't have to pretend; I don't have to compete. I can be me. There is something intrinsically freeing about being authentically you.

I suppose the beauty of North Dakota is also in its people. Some say that because of their Germanic and Norwegian roots these Dakotans are stoic and cold. Yes, they are reserved, but they are sincere. These are hardy people who have toiled the lands for generations, who have braved the elements year by year, surviving crop failures and economic disasters and the storms of life. Indeed they are stoic, but cold they are not. They are warm hearted and generous.

I think what I love the most about Dakotans is that they are unpretentious.

I have met rich people in my lifetime. Some of them enjoy displaying their wealth for all to see. Not so with Dakotans. The oil has made some people in our state wealthy, and yet you would never know it because they maintain the simplicity of the lifestyle that made them Dakotans in the first place. They are authentic people, true to themselves.

The plains are a type of monastic space where you can breathe deeply and listen to the sound of your own breath. We have driven on quiet country roads where we have not seen a person or a car for a hundred miles and the beauty is unique and unspoiled. It is a different kind of loveliness—no majestic mountains to make you gasp in wonder, no ocean or sea breezes to tantalize your senses. Instead, merely a simple, almost austere, reclusive beauty that allows you to experience God. Simple serenity! It is a cloistered space where people can draw aside, reflect, pray, and prepare themselves to serve God.

In the evening, when we go walking, we can hear the wind blowing and the birds singing in the trees. There is no discordant city noise to drown out the melody from God's creation. We can watch the wild grass quiver in the breeze while the western sky captivates us—the blushes of ruby red, the rosy tinges—before the sun slips away for the night. No urban smog, no skyscrapers, no concrete jungle, only rare and unspoiled beauty. You are filled with a sure hope that on the morrow the sun will rise in the eastern sky, delighting you once again with glorious shades and colors that will surprise you and leave you breathless.

We live in a world that is desperate for hope—a hurting world, a sad world. As young men and women draw aside to this serene and barren space, they can sit, wait, and listen in the quietness and solitude to hear God speak.

Many of these devoted young people will go from this monastic stillness to the towns of India, the villages of China, the mountains of Nepal, the plains of Mongolia, and the hustle and bustle of cities around the globe. They will encounter broken and empty lives on their journey, and they will meet desperate hurting people and children. But because they have experienced the quiet stillness of the plains of North Dakota, and because they have withdrawn and retreated to the unique space and place of Trinity Bible College, they will go into this broken world with confidence. No, it is not the bold arrogance of youthfulness, but quiet confidence in Jesus that fills them with certainty and resolve to take wild hope to a broken world.

Thank you for taking the time to read the pilgrim journey of a simple South African girl who encountered Jesus and had her life turned upside down and inside out. I have written this book from my heart. I have cried and laughed as I have remembered. But above all, I have sat in quiet reflection and said thank you to a God who has blessed my life immeasurably.

And now, as I end this page, I am already anticipating the next one in our lives. My love for Jesus cannot be explained in words because no amount of adjectives could do justice in describing His beauty and my immense love for Him.

I am devoted to Paul, the most incredible human being I know and the kindest and most loving man I could ever have wished to journey with. Together our hearts are filled with wild hope for this season of our lives.

Jay is now living in Los Angeles, California. I am happy to say that he is completely recovered. He suffered with Crohn's for eight long years, but his disease is now in remission. He still bears horrendous scars from surgery, but they are a reminder of our amazing God and His gracious hand on Jay's life.

Our darling Anna and her husband Rich live in Charlotte, North Carolina, and have given us two of the most incredible gifts we could ever have hoped for.

What can I say about our two grandchildren, Ava Carol and Tylan Alexander? They have given Paul and me more joy than we deserve and have both crept into our hearts. They have both of us firmly wrapped around their little fingers. We look forward to hundreds more sleepovers, eating popcorn and watching *My Little Pony, Fireman Sam, Thomas Tank* and *Olivia*. Granddad will keep his hoard of liquorice for the two of them so that all three of them can eat when no one is looking. We will watch them grow and support them as they become everything God has destined for them to be.

My prayer is that your life has been touched and enriched by my story. Above all, I trust that every heart has been inspired to wild hope in Jesus.

Look up my friend—wild geese are on the horizon and spring is on its way!

I am and always will be, recklessly abandoned, ruthlessly committed, and in relentless pursuit of Jesus,

Carol Alexander

Paul and me with my wonderful parents and grandchildren in 2012.

Paul and Jay both now strong and healthy. I am grateful every day of my life that they are both still with me.

My brother, Geoff, and his family and Paul's niece Laura all visit us in Charlotte in December 2013.

Happy moments with my two precious grandchildren, Ava and Tylan.

Ava and Tylan fill my life with so much joy.

CPSIA information can be obtained at www.ICGtesting.com
Printed in the USA
LVOW07s1103010815

448397LV00002B/2/P